The Magnificat

Musicians As Biblical Interpreters

MADONNA DEL PARTO (1460?)
by Piero della Francesca
Cappella del Cimitero, Monterchi (Tuscany)

Scala—Firenze, Editione del Commune di Sansepolcro

The Magnificat

Musicians As Biblical Interpreters

by
SAMUEL TERRIEN

illustrated by Bruce Gebert

PAULIST PRESS
New York/Mahwah, NJ

Cover design by Moe Berman.
Author photo courtesy of Cécile Terrien Lampton.

Library of Congress Cataloging-in-Publication Data

Terrien, Samuel L., 1911–
     The Magnificat: musicians as Biblical interpreters/by Samuel
Terrien.
          p.   cm.
     Includes bibliographical references and index.
     ISBN 0-8091-3485-3 (paper)
     1. Magnificat—Criticism, interpretation, etc.   2. Magnificat
(Music)—History and criticism.   I. Title.
BV199.C32M33   1995
226.4'06—dc20   94-34748
                                                                              CIP

Published by Paulist Press
997 Macarthur Boulevard
Mahwah, New Jersey 07430

Printed and bound in the
United States of America

Table of Contents

Strophe II

Recorded Musical Illustrations

Grand Magnificat in D Major
"Symphonia; Magnificat; Et exultavit"

Wiener Akademie Chor, Stuttgart Chamber Orchestra
Karl Münchinger   London OS 26103

5.   *Alan Hovhaness* (b. 1911), New York

Magnificat for Solo Voices, Op. 157
"Celestial Fanfare; Magnificat; Et exultavit"

Louisville Orchestra, U. of Louisville Choir
Robert Whitney   Lou-614

STROPHE TWO
THE COMPASSION OF GOD

1.   *Marc-Antoine Charpentier* (1634–1704), Paris, Versailles

Grand Magnificat for eight voices
"Magnificat; Et misericordia"

Chorale des Jeunesses musicales de France, Orchestre
Jean-François Paillard—Louis Martini   Vanguard BJ-663

2.   *Antonio Vivaldi* (1678–1741), Venice

Magnificat in B Minor
"Et misericordia"

Orchestra da Camera dell'Angelicum
Ruggero Maghini Angelicum   LP A5917

3. *Johann Sebastian Bach* (1685–1750), Leipzig

Grand Magnificat in D Major
"Et misericordia"

Choir and Orchestra of the Vienna State Opera
Felix Prohaska   HM. 22SD

4. *Carl Philipp Emanuel Bach* (1717–1788), Potsdam, Hamburg

Magnificat in D Major
"Et misericordia"

Akademie Chor and Vienna State Opera Orchestra
Felix Prohaska   Vanguard BB 516-B

STROPHE THREE
THE MOTHER OF REVOLUTION

1. *Claudio Monteverdi* (1567–1643), Mantua

Magnificat a 6 voci
"Fecit potentiam; Deposuit"

Kantorei Barmen-Gemarke
Helmut Kahlhöfer—Barenreiter Musicaphon   BM 30L 1307

2. *Johann Sebastian Bach* (1685-1750), Leipzig

Grand Magnificat in D Major
"Fecit potentiam; Deposuit"

Chor der Deutschen Oper Berlin, Berliner Philharmoniker
Herbert Von Karajan   Deutsche Grammophon 2531 048

3. *Michael Tippett* (b. 1905), London, Cambridge

"My Soul Doth Magnify"

St. John's College,
Cambridge—George Guest   Argo RG 340

4. *Alan Hovhaness* (b. 1911), New York

"Fecit potentiam"

Louisville Orchestra,
U. of Louisville Choir—Robert Whitney   Lou-614

5. *Krzysztof Penderecki* (b. 1933), Cracow and New Haven

"Fecit Potentiam"

Polish Radio Chorus
and Orchestra—K. Penderecki   Angel S-37141

STROPHE FOUR
THE SACRALITY OF THE FUTURE

1. *Andrea Gabrieli* (1510–1586), Venice

"Suscepit Israel"

The Ambrosian Singers—Denis Stevens   Angel S-36443

2. *Johann Sebastian Bach* (1685–1750), Leipzig

Grand Magnificat in D Major
"Suscepit Israel"

Chorale Philippe Caillart, Orchestre de chambre de la
Radiodiffusion Sarroise—Karl Ristenpart   Erato LDE 3333

3. *Giovanni-Battista Sammartini* (1701–1775), Venice

Magnificat in G Major
"Suscepit Israel"

Orchestra da Camera dell'Angelicum, Coro polifonico
di Milano—Umberto Cattini Musica Sacra
Düsseldorf AMS 13

4. *Carl Philipp Emanuel Bach* (1717–1788), Potsdam, Hamburg

"Suscepit Israel"

King's College, Cambridge—Academy of St. Martin-in-the-
Fields—Philip Ledger   Argo ZRG 853

POSTSCRIPT

5. *Johann Sebastian Bach* (1685–1750), Leipzig

Grand Magnificat in D Major
"Gloria"

Philippe Caillart Chorus, Pro Arte Chamber Orchestra
of Munich—Kurt Redel   Erato XWN 18465

For Sammy and Cara

Preface

The Magnificat was originally a Hebrew psalm, sung with instrumental accompaniment. From the Middle Ages to the present, the various modes of Byzantine, Ambrosian, Gregorian and Anglican chant have made it a sublime element of the liturgy.

Nonetheless, for many contemporary listeners this traditional manner of singing sounds somewhat horizontal, remote and abstract for the rendering of the text. During the fourteenth century, when the Ars Nova introduced the use of polyphony and instrumentation, choral and orchestral settings were composed. In Renaissance, Baroque, Romantic and modern styles, musicians have not only provided innovative ways of singing the poem, but they have also expounded musically the meaning of the text more forcefully than scholars and theological commentators have often done.

This book seeks to present, not for musicologists but for enlightened worshippers, an illumination of the poem in the light of recent scholarship, together with the interpretation of the text through selected musical excerpts from the greatest compositions of the Magnificat during the past six centuries.

When musical genius presides over the espousal of speech and tone, rhythm and sound-color, the synthesis amounts to a veritable explosion of sense. Music and words supported by instruments can create a third medium of expressiveness that enhances both the esthetic and the serene sharpness of spirituality.

To the ministers, priests, priors and sisters-general of monastic communities, presidents of various theological seminaries and officials of the Hymn Society of America who have invited me to lecture on the musical exegesis of the Magnificat in their institutions or national gatherings, and to the many individuals who have offered critical comments, I here express my deep gratitude.

The librarians of Union Theological Seminary, the Music Library of Columbia University, the Andover-Newton School of Theology and the Harvard Divinity School have offered numerous courtesies beyond normal stewardship.

For their wisdom and fortitude, a debt is also owed to those who patiently reviewed, typed and retyped the manuscript: Sara Frantz Terrien, Cécile Terrien Lampton and Stephanie Adams. A special word of thanks is herewith extended to Alys Terrien-Queen, of the New England Conservatory of Music, and the Rev. Dr. Alexander C. Post, composer and Minister of Music at the First Unitarian Church in San Francisco, California, for sharing with me their musical knowledge and insights.

My gratitude also goes to Professor Denis Stevens, President of the Accademia Monteverdiana, Santa Barbara, California, who many years ago expounded for me the subtleties of Renaissance music. Even today I remember with keen appreciation the late Robert S. Tangeman, who taught musicology at the School of Sacred Music, Union Theological Seminary. We had together many fruitful conversations about the settings of the Magnificat.

In his *Tales of the Hasidim*, Martin Buber reports that Rabbi Pinhas said in one of his prayers:

> Lord of the world, if I could sing,
> I should not let you remain up above.
> I should harry you with my song
> Until you came down and stayed here with us.*

These words may describe the theology of The Magnificat.

S.T.

---

* Martin Buber, *Tales of the Hasidim*, tr. Olga Marx (New York: Schocken Books, 1947), p. 125.

Introduction

The Magnificat is the song which, according to the gospel of Luke (1:44–55), Mary sang to Elizabeth. After the future mother of John the Baptist had greeted the future mother of Jesus by saying,

Blessed art thou among women (vs 42),

Mary replied by singing,

My whole being proclaims the greatness of the Lord
(vs 46).

I

The song of Mary is similar to the song of Hannah, future mother of the prophet Samuel (1 Sam 2:1–10), and its form resembles that of many ancient psalms.

Because it evokes the history of Hebrew-Christian faith from Abraham to the end of time, it has been described as a biblical theology in miniature. Modern church activists see it as a call to revolution. However that may be, the song brings together the esthetics of divine worship and the ethics of human service.

II

Like the rest of the New Testament to which it belongs, the text of the Magnificat is preserved in Greek. Was it, however, originally sung in Hebrew? The issue is not one of idle erudition, for the question of language affects the determination of the poem's strophic structure, the meaning of its key words, and the movement of its thought.

For years, scholars have debated the authorship, composition, and original language of the Magnificat.[1] Exegetes have examined the various conjectures with critical care. The first chapter of this book proposes an hypothesis which sheds a new light on some of its cryptic lines, and thus may clarify the theology of the poet.

III

Eastern churches sing the Magnificat in Greek, Coptic, Syriac, Ethiopic, and other ancient or modern languages, at the morning service of Lauds. Western Christendom intones it at Vespers (Evensong). For many centuries its Latin version was chanted on Gregorian modes. It is now sung in English and other modern tongues.

With the rise of polyphonic music in the Late Middle Ages, and especially during the Renaissance and the Baroque period, numerous artists have set the Magnificat for voices—solo or chorus—organ and orchestral instruments. Out of several hundred of such compositions, about fifty are outstanding and are now available in recordings, from the Ars Nova *Magnificat* of Johannes de Quatris, ca. 1350, to the modern *Magnificat* of Krzysztov Penderecki composed in 1972.

A few selections will reveal the attentiveness to detail with which these musicians have pondered the biblical text.

IV

Liturgy is a communal act of adoration, but worship begins and ends in solitariness. A structural analysis of the Magnificat shows that it was composed by a single poet, and a minute examination of its text reveals that it covers the whole sweep of Hebrew-Christian faith. It

---

[1] The most extensive bibliography is to be found in Alberto Valentini, *Il Magnificat: Genere letterario, Struttura, Esegesi* (Bologna: Editizioni Dehoniane Bologna, 1987), pp. 259–274; F. Boron, *L'évangile selon Saint Luc . . .* (Genève, 1991), pp. 80–81.

also propels it to the horizon of humanity. At the same time, it bears the marks of an intimate exposure to what Keats called "solitary things: such as dodge conception at the very bourne of heaven."[2] The song attributed to Mary sprang from the exultation of an individual steeped within the collective exaltation of the nascent church.

---

[2] Cited by Helen Vendler, "Married to Hurry and Grim Song," *The New Yorker Magazine*, July 27, 1987, p. 74.

Table I

The Magnificat

I

46. My whole being proclaims the greatness of the Lord,
47. And my spirit is thrilled in God my Savior,

48. For he has regarded the low estate of his woman slave;
Thus, behold! All generations henceforth will sing my
happiness.

II

49. For the Potent One has done to me great things,
And his name is the Holy One!

50. And his compassion goes to those who fear him
From generation to generation.

CORE-VERSE

51. He has shown strength in his arm;
He has scattered the proud in the imagination of their
hearts.

III

52. He has put down potentates from their thrones,
And he has exalted those of low estate;

53. He has filled the hungry with good things,
And the rich he has sent empty away.

IV

54. He has upheld Israel his boy slave
In remembrance of his compassion,

55. As he spoke to our fathers,
Abraham, and his seed, forever.

The Magnificat

I

46. Magnificat anima mea Dominum:
47. et exultavit spiritus meus in Deo salutari meo.
48. Quia respexit humilitatem ancillae suae:
     ecce ex hoc beatam me dicent omnes generationes.

II

49. Quia fecit mihi magna qui potens est:
     et sanctum nomen eius.
50. Et misericordia eius a progenie in progenies
     timentibus eum.

51. Fecit potentiam in brachio suo:
     dispersit superbos mente cordis sui.

III

52. Deposuit potentes de sede,
     et exaltavit humiles.
53. Esurientes implevit bonis:
     et divites dimisit inanes.

IV

54. Suscepit Israel puerum suum,
     recordatus misericordiae suae.
55. Sicut locutus est ad patres nostros,
     Abraham, et semini eius in saecula.

Seated Virgin

Chapter 1

A Masterpiece of Hebrew Psalmody

The Magnificat is a tightly knit psalm of a form and style comparable to those of the so-called Psalms of David in the Old Testament. It is composed of four strophes (Luke 1:46–53). These are coupled in pairs (see Table I) and articulated around a central distich or core-verse (vs 51).[1]

Within the context of the infancy narrative (Luke 1:5–2:52), the Magnificat binds the hope of Israel to the birth of Jesus.

I. COMPOSITION

Most scholars, Roman Catholic as well as Protestant, now regard the Magnificat as a hymn of the early church, but opinions differ concerning its authorship, its social environment, and its original language.

1. Conservative Greek Orthodox and Roman Catholics, together with Protestant fundamentalists and evangelicals, still attribute the poem to Mary.[2] They argue that the family of Jesus played a part in the primitive community of Christians in Jerusalem (Acts 1:4, 13–14, etc.), and that Mary may well have told the disciples assembled in the Upper Room her reminiscences of the birth and infancy of Jesus. Without accepting the validity of fantastic legends that appeared in

---

[1] Numerous hymns of the Psalter present a similar structure.

[2] See J. Gresham Machen, *The Virgin Birth of Christ* (New York: Harper, 1930), pp. 95–97; Lucien Deiss, *Mary, Daughter of Sion*, tr. B.T. Blair (Collegeville, Minnesota, 1972), pp. 106–126; René Laurentin, *Les Évangiles de l'enfance du Christ* (Paris: Desclée de Brouwer, 1982), pp. 13–24; 445–449; 451; 543–544.

1

later centuries, one may reasonably conjecture that the mother of Jesus was deeply religious, exceptionally gifted, and well-versed in the hymnbook of the synagogue. Within the context of the annunciation and of the visitation, the Magnificat breathes the ebullience of a pregnant woman, convinced that the new life she carried in her womb would affect the destiny of all humankind (Luke 1:48). Might, then, the Magnificat have been composed by Mary?

It is unlikely that a young woman of Galilee, presumably of humble origin, would have been allowed to master the complex techniques of psalmody which the choirmasters of the ancient kings of Judah had inherited from Canaanite, Egyptian and Akkadian cultic poets. Furthermore, all the songs of the infancy narrative bear identical affinities of style, syntax, and prosodic devices. They also deal with themes which point to the same embryonic Christology, typical of the early Judeo-Christian church. If Mary had composed the Magnificat, we should also subscribe to the absurd conclusion that she was responsible for Elizabeth's *Benedicta* (Luke 1:42-45), Zechariah's *Benedictus* (1:68-79), and Simeon's *Nunc Dimittis* (2:29-32).

2. Several scholars believe that the author of Luke-Acts wrote all the canticles as well as the apostolic speeches of the first part of the book of Acts (1-15). Such a view is hardly acceptable, for these hymns and discourses, while written in Greek, contain a number of Semitisms (Hebrew or Aramaic) that are not found elsewhere in the Lukan literature.[3]

3. A number of exegetes[4] are inclined to maintain that the Lukan writer borrowed the Magnificat as well as the other canticles of the infancy narrative from a purely Jewish, non-Christian, background. To sustain this conjecture, they point out that this hymn merely praises the God of Israel, the traditional upholder of social justice. The author

---

[3] See discussion on the origin of the Magnificat in Stephen Farris, *The Hymns of Luke's Infancy Narratives: Their Origin, Meaning and Significance, Journal for the Study of the New Testament*, Supplement Series 9 (Sheffield, 1985), pp. 14-30.

[4] Friedrich Spitta, "Das Magnificat, ein Psalm der Maria und nicht der Elisabeth," *Festgabe . . . H.J. Holtzmann* (Tübingen: Mohr, 1892), pp. 63-64; Hermann Gunkel, "Die Lieder in der Kindheitsgeschichte Jesu bei Lukas," *Festgabe . . . A. von Harnack* (Tübingen: Mohr, 1921), pp. 60-61; Paul Winter, "Magnificat and Benedictus—Maccabaean Psalms?" *John Rylands Library Bulletin*, XXXVII (1954-55), pp. 328-47.

of the gospel adopted this theme eagerly for it suited his concern for the poor and the oppressed, and he inserted in this Jewish song an extra doublet or *bicolon* on Mary's happiness (vs 48) in order to adapt it for his specific context of the infancy narrative.

Such a view ignores the strophic integrity and the compactness of the entire poem (again see Table I), which balances the theme of God's slave-woman (vs 48) with that of God's slave-boy (vs 54).

4. Still other interpreters[5] propose that the Lukan writer used not a strictly Jewish but a Jewish-Christian source. In the course of its services of informal worship, the early community in Jerusalem may well have rehearsed oral traditions and psalmodic sequences that would have initiated the motifs of Abraham and the fathers (vss 54-55), unless these motifs belonged already to an earlier material.

The primitive Jerusalem church was constituted by women and men of Jewish origin (Acts 1:12-14; 4:24b-30; 12:2) and it included members of the Jewish sect of the *Anawim*, "The Poor" in the spiritual as well as material sense of the word. Not unlike the members of the Qumran community who wrote the Dead Sea Scrolls, the *Anawim* tended to renounce the earthly world while passionately waiting for the world to come. They hailed from a long tradition of soberness and even destitution amply celebrated by the ancient psalmists.[6]

Since the mother of Jesus was apparently present at the Upper Room (Acts 1:12-14), she may well have inspired some of the earliest Christian poets who had mastered the intricacies of psalmodic versification.

---

[5] Sigmund Mowinckel, *The Psalms in Israel's Worship*, Tr. D.R. Ap-Thomas (New York: Abingdon, 1964), pp. 122-23; Douglas R. Jones, "The Background and Character of the Lukan Psalms," *Journal of Theological Studies*, XIX (1968), pp. 19-50; Heinz Schürmann, *Das Lukasevangelium* (Freiburg A.M.: Herder, 1969), I, pp. 70-80; Raymond E. Brown, *The Birth of the Messiah* (Garden City, NY: Doubleday, 1977), pp. 346-50; Joseph A. Fitzmyer, *The Gospel According to Luke I-IX* (Garden City, NY: Doubleday, 1983), pp. 361-62.

[6] Alfred Rahlfs, *Ani und Anaw in den Psalmen* (Leipzig: Dietrich, 1892); Harris Birkeland, *Ani und Anaw in den Psalmen* (Oslo: Dybwad, 1933); P. van den Berge, "'ani et 'anaw dans les Psaumes," *Le Psautier*, R. de Langhe, ed. (Louvain: Université, 1962), pp. 273-95; Albert Gelin, *Les pauvres de Yahweh* (Paris: Cerf, 1956); Raymond Martin-Achard, "Yahweh et les Anawim," *Theologische Zeitschrift*, XXI (1965), pp. 349-57; R.E. Brown, *op. cit*, pp. 352-55.

II. ORIGINAL LANGUAGE

Was the Magnificat first composed in Greek, as preserved in the gospel of Luke, or was it translated orally from a Semitic original now lost? The question is important, for the elucidation of its key words and the determination of its rhythmic movement depend in no small measure upon consonantal and vocalic sounds as well as upon the semantic overtones of its vocabulary. Obviously, the analysis of a Petrarchan or Shakespearean sonnet could not be made on the basis of a German or French translation.

In the first century A.D., Jews of Galilee and even of Judea spoke Aramaic and also Greek.[7] A few scholars have suggested that the Magnificat was composed in Aramaic,[8] but no philological evidence sustains this claim. Other scholars believe that the Magnificat was composed in Greek and that the Lukan text as we have it represents the original text.[9] However, if the Magnificat was composed within the early Jewish-Christian community of Jerusalem, its language was most probably Hebrew.[10]

---

[7] W. Chomsky, "What Was the Jewish Vernacular during the Second Commonwealth?" *Jewish Quarterly Review*, XLII (1951–52), pp. 193–212; Jehoshua M. Grintz, "Hebrew as a Spoken Language in the Last Days of the Second Temple," *Journal of Biblical Literature*, LXXXIII (1964), pp. 404–08.

[8] Matthew Black, *An Aramaic Approach to the Gospels and Acts* (Oxford: Clarendon, 1954), pp. 111–13.

[9] Adolf von Harnack, "Das Magnificat der Elisabeth (Lke 1:46–55) nebst einigen Bemerkungen zu Luk 1 und 2," *Sitzungsberichte der preussischen Akademie*, XXVII (1900), pp. 638–56; H.F.D. Sparks, "The Semitisms of St. Luke's Gospel," *Journal of Theological Studies*, XLIV (1943), pp. 129–38; M.-D. Gouler and M. L. Sanderson, "St. Luke's Genesis," *Journal of Theological Studies*, VIII (1957), pp. 12–13, 20–22; N. Turner, "The Relation of Luke I and II to Hebraic Sources and the Rest of Luke-Acts," *New Testament Studies*, II (1955–56), pp. 100–09; Robert C. Tannehill, "The Magnificat as a Poem," *Journal of Biblical Literature*, XCIII (1974), pp. 263–75; Paul Bemile, *The Magnificat within the Context and Framework of Lukan Theology* (Frankfurt a.-M.: Lang, 1986), pp. 37–62.

[10] R.A. Aytoun, "The Ten Lukan Hymns of the Nativity in Their Original Language," *Journal of Theological Studies*, XVIII (1917), pp. 281–83; René Laurentin, "Traces d'allusions étymologiques dans Luc 1–2," *Biblica*, XXXVII (1956), pp. 437–39; XXXVIII (1957), pp. 15–17; *Structure et théologie de Luc I–II* (Paris: Gabalda, 1957), pp. 12–13, 82–86; Jones, *op. cit.*, pp. 19–50; P. Boyd Mather, "The Search for the Living Text of the Lucan Infancy Narrative," *The Living Text: Essays in Honor of Ernest W. Saunders*, Dennis E. Groh and Robert Jewett, eds. (Lanham, Maryland: University Press of America, 1985), pp. 129–30.

Pious Jews in Roman times had not lost the use of the Hebrew language. They read the scripture—Torah and Nebiyim, the Law and the Prophets—in Hebrew. On sabbaths and festivals they sang the Psalms in Hebrew. It may well be that Jesus taught his disciples Hebrew prayers and Hebrew summaries of his teaching, like the Beatitudes, and other poetic sequences now gathered in the sermon on the mount. In fact, the Magnificat includes—as it will be seen later—several quotations from the Psalms. Many features suggest the hypothesis of a Hebrew original. To be sure, Semitisms in Greek documents of this period do not necessarily demonstrate that such documents were translated from the Hebrew, because a Jewish or Jewish-Christian poet, whose mother tongue was Hebrew or Aramaic, would have easily introduced into the Greek language he used a number of grammatical and generally stylistic habits inherited unconsciously from his family background.   .

The advocates of a Greek original point out that the quotations from the Psalms were made not from the Hebrew but from the Greek version of the Septuagint. This fact, however, does not imply that the poem was originally composed in Greek, since any translator would have been conversant with the Septuagint, and would have used this version rather than have tried to offer his own rendering of passages as well-known as those of the Psalms. The following examples of Semitisms, among others, can hardly be explained except as indications of a Hebrew poem.[11]

The absence of verbs in verses 49b and 50a ("The Holy One . . . his name" and "his compassion . . . to generations") betrays a Hebrew idiomatic usage by which the verbal copulative "is" between subject and predicate does not need to appear.

Again, the sudden occurrence of tenses from the Greek present to the Greek aorist in "and exults" (vs 47) does not denote a time shift between the first stich and the second but betrays the literal rendering

---

[11] R. A. Martin, "Some Syntactical Criteria of Translation Greek," *Vetus Testamentum*, X (1960), pp. 295–310; S. C. Farris, "On Discerning Semitic Sources in Lk 1-2," in R. T. France, et al., *Gospel Perspectives* (Sheffield: University Press, 1981), pp. 201-237, *id.*, *The Hymns . . . (op. cit.)*, pp. 31-62.

of the idiomatic practice, common in Hebrew, of what used to be called "the consecutive imperfect."

Moreover, several alliterative correspondences, which will be studied in the course of the strophic analysis, would not be noticed in the Greek, but they are evident in the Hebrew.

Reconstitution of the canticle of Mary in Hebrew has been successfully carried out by several scholars thoroughly acquainted with the Hebrew Bible and the Septuagintal Greek Bible.[12]

III. STROPHIC STRUCTURE

The strophic structures published to date may be listed as follows:

1. Some scholars divide the song into two strophes. The first is deemed to be a psalm of personal thanksgiving, while the second (vss 51–53) is usually called an eschatological hymn, dealing with the world to come.[13]

2. Others propose a sequence of three short thanksgiving psalms: first, a song of individual praise (vss 46–50); second, a canticle of the poor (vss 51–53); and third, a national hymn (vss 54–55).[14]

3. The majority of recent writers suggest a four-strophe division (vss 46–48; 49–50; 51–53; 54–55), although precise proposals of strophic structure may vary.[15]

---

[12] The Greek gospels of Luke and John were translated into Hebrew by Giovanni Battista in 1668, and his version was revised by Thomas Yeates in 1805, published anew by Jean Carmignac, *Évangiles de Luc et Jean* (Tournai: Brepols, 1982). Cf. *id.*, "Studies in the Hebrew Background of the Synoptic Gospels," *Annual of the Swedish Institute of Theology*, VII (1968–69), pp. 64–93. The subsequent analysis is partially based on the translations of the New Testament in Hebrew by Franz Delitzsch (1888) and David Ginsburg (1901). Such a linguistic reconstitution brings to light a remarkable number of semantic nuances not discernible in the Greek.

[13] Schürmann, *op. cit.*, pp. 70–72. A two-strophe structure with different divisions (vss 46–49; 50–55) is favored by Augustin George, *L'annonce du salut de Dieu: Lecture de l'évangile de Luc* (Paris: Equiptes Enseignantes, 1963), pp. 174–75. Other critics treat the whole poem as a unit but in effect divide it into two parts; see Tannehill, *op. cit.*, pp. 263–75; D. Minguez, "Poética generativa del Magnificat," *Biblica*, LXI (1980), pp. 56–75.

[14] Leonardus Ramaroson, "Ad Structuram 'Magnificat,'" *Biblica*, LXI (1980), pp. 56–75; cf. Baron, *op. cit.*, pp. 84–85.

[15] Paul Gaechter, *Maria im Erdenleben* (Innsbruck: Tyrolia, 1954), pp. 293–94; Jacques Dupont, "Le Magnificat comme discours sur Dieu," *Nouvelle Revue Théologique*, CII (1980), pp. 421–43. Some scholars prefer to divide the poem in two strophes (vss 48–50; 52–53), pre-

4. Apparently, on account of the distinct meanings of the five sentences in the poem, a few scholars have advocated a five-strophe structure (vss 46–47; 48–49; 50–51; 52–53; 54–55).[16] Such a division, like the others, disregards the fluidity of the thematic motifs that are anticipated, explicitly treated, and later alluded to, in a practice common to ancient Hebrew poetry, especially in the Psalms and in the poem of Job.

When the Greek text of the Magnificat is translated into Hebrew, several striking features appear: not only parallelism of key words but also consonantal or vocalic examples of alliteration (see Table II).

1. The core-verse (vs 51) is so designated because it provides the central articulation for the entire poem. It looks at once *backward* to Strophes I and II (vs 51a, "the might of God's arm") and *forward* to Strophes III and IV (vs 51b, "the scattering of the proud").

2. The noun "great-things" (vs 49a, in Strophe II, *gedôlôt*) is a cognate of the initial verb of Strophe I (vs 46a), "proclaims greatness" (*giddelah*). The theme of greatness sets the tone for the whole Magnificat. In addition, the verb of the second stich of Strophe I, "and exults" (*wattagel*), offers a consonantal alliteration with the motif of greatness (vs 47).

3. The word "his-woman-slave" (*shiphchatô*) in Strophe I (vs 48a) is paralleled, deflected, and amplified by the word "his-slave-boy" (*'abdô*) at the opening of the concluding Strophe IV (vs 54a). The transforming parallelism provides the major semantic rhythm of the poem, for it unites the mother-to-be—the slave-woman of the Lord—with the slave-boy of the Lord, whose identification with Israel—"the slave of the Lord" (Isa 41:7, etc.)—is now transferred to the expected child. This feature, above all the others, determines the theological purpose of the Magnificat, which is to broaden the mystery of the incarnation into the mystery of the people of God, and vice versa: Israel is incarnate in Jesus.

4. The divine actor is praised by the expectant mother (vss

---

ceded by an Introduction (vss 46–47), followed by a Conclusion (vss 54–55). This amounts in fact to a division in four strophes. See Brown, *op. cit.*, pp. 358–59; Fitzmyer, *op. cit.*, p.360.

[16] Jean-Marie Lagrange, *Évangile selon saint Luc* (Paris: Gabalda, 1948), pp. 45–51; S. Farris, *The Hymns* (*op. cit.*), pp. 113–116.

Table II

Thematic Articulation

(Parallelisms and Assonances of Hebrew Key Words)

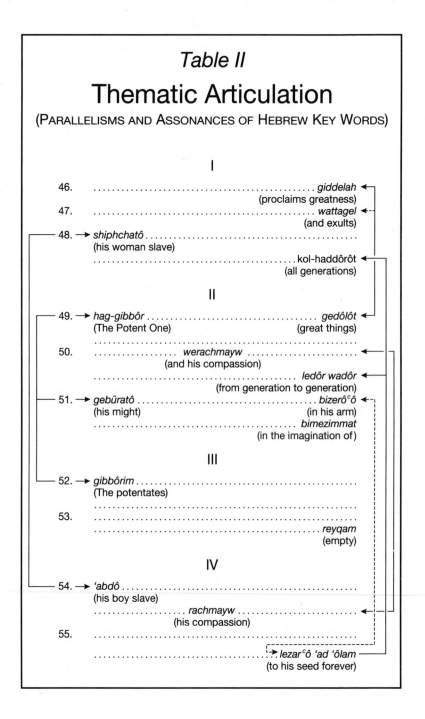

I

46. . . . . *giddelah*
(proclaims greatness)

47. . . . . *wattagel*
(and exults)

48. *shiphchatô* . . . .
(his woman slave)

. . . . *kol-haddôrôt*
(all generations)

II

49. *hag-gibbôr* . . . . *gedôlôt*
(The Potent One)   (great things)

50. . . . . *werachmayw* . . . .
(and his compassion)

. . . . *ledôr wadôr*
(from generation to generation)

51. *gebûratô* . . . . *bizerô°ô*
(his might)   (in his arm)

. . . . *bimezimmat*
(in the imagination of)

III

52. *gibbôrim* . . . .
(The potentates)

. . . .

53. . . . .

. . . . *reyqam*
(empty)

IV

54. *'abdô* . . . .
(his boy slave)

. . . . *rachmayw* . . . .
(his compassion)

55. . . . .

. . . . *lezar°ô 'ad 'ôlam*
(to his seed forever)

46–47) because he is hailed as both "The Potent One" and "The Almighty One" (*hag-gibbôr*) in Strophe II (vs 49*a*). Within the context of the annunciation and the visitation, the noun *gibbôr*, "hero," receives a double meaning: the hero is the sovereign ruler of history and also the initiator of the birth. It is no accident that the name of the angel who announces to Mary the unique grace that is bestowed upon her is called "Gabriel" (Lk 1:26 ff.). This theophoric name is formed with the verb *gabar*, "to be powerful," from which the nouns *geber*, "he-man," and *gibbôr*, "hero," are derived. The name "Gabriel" literally means "God is potent."

5. The same word *gibbôr* ("mighty one") reappears in Strophe III as a plural noun *gibbôrim*, "potentates" (vs 52*a*), whom the Potent One will unseat from their thrones.

6. The motif of "his might" or "his potency" (*gebûratô*) is insisted upon and even reinforced in the same sentence by the use of the expression "by his arm" (*bizerô῾ô*), for the core-verse (vs 51) binds together that which precedes with that which follows not only because it evokes divine initiative in the conception of Jesus but also because it prepares the divine judgment by which the potentates and the rich are going to be dispossessed and thrown into the void (Strophe III, vss 52–53).

7. The core-verse assumes an additional function, for the expression *bizerô῾ô*, "by his arm," forms a paranomasia with *lezarô*, "to his seed," at the very end of the poem in Strophe IV (vs 55*b*). The two nouns are homonymous, although not cognated. The roots of the two nouns *zeroa῾* ("arm") and *zera῾* ("seed") are identically written, yet these homonymous verbal roots are actually distinct, as shown by comparative Semitics. The consonantal pun was unmistakably considered to be a sign of poetic elegance as well as a ground for exegetical meditation. What is the relationship between the divine begetting and the posterity of Abraham? The theological purpose of the incarnation— the people of God—receives a secondary stress.

8. A further feature appears in the antithesis which, within the core-verse (vs 51) opposes God's arm (vs 51*a*) to the "vain imagination" of the proud (vs 51*b*). It is this antithesis which both introduces the reversal of social injustice in Strophe III and ends with the word *reyqam*, "empty" (vs 53*b*).

It may be concluded that the Magnificat was originally a Hebrew poem, which the author of the third gospel, or the oral tradition he followed, incorporated into the narrative of the infancy. It is artistically constructed. The use of key words binds together the various parts from strophe to strophe. As the themes are introduced into new contexts, the song of Mary amplifies its sweep from individual happiness to the ongoingness of world history.[17]

---

[17] Recent studies stress the importance of the analysis of the form in order to understand the meaning. See Jean Delorme, "Le magnificat: la forme et le sens," in *La vie de la Parole*: *De l'Ancien au Nouveau Testament, études d'exégèse et d'herméneutique bibliques offertes à Pierre Grelot* (Paris: Desclée, 1987), pp. 175–194.

Chapter 2

The First Daughter of the Church

46. My soul doth magnify the Lord,
47. And my spirit hath rejoiced in God my Savior.

48. For he hath regarded the low estate of his
    handmaiden:
    For, behold, from henceforth all generations shall
    call me blessed.

I. THE GRANDEUR

The word "Magnificat" which opens the hymn and has given its title to it is traditionally rendered "doth magnify." In contemporary English, this verb implies a factitive or causative sense. It evokes the connotation of a magnifying glass, by which a small object is made visible to the human eye through enlargement. In Elizabethan English as well as in Latin, Greek, and Hebrew, the word "magnify" was used in a declarative and intensive sense. It meant "to esteem greatly," or "to celebrate the greatness of," "to bring out in song and ritual gesture, possibly in dance, the divine grandeur."

Obviously, a human singer cannot make God great. The realm of infinity transcends the finiteness of a human being, even the mother-to-be of the Holy Child.

From the start, we are introduced to the ancient poetry of the Hebrew Psalter, in which cultic poets invited their congregation to

11

join them in a celebration of divine transcendence. This celebration is
immediately linked with the call to exalt the divine name. This motif
will come in the second strophe of the Magnificat (vs 49). But in the
Psalms, the two themes are interrelated without pause:

> O magnify the Lord with me,
> And let us exalt his name together! (Ps 34:3 [Heb 4])

The singer of the Magnificat does not, however, summon others
to participate in this act of praise. The tone is intensely personal. It
concerns the intimate confession of a young woman who shares the
secret of her own inner life with another woman of her circle. She is
bound to her by affection and a common, somewhat different, but
physically similar, destiny. Elizabeth is pregnant with the future John
the Baptist.

At once, we discover that the influence of the prayerbook of Israel
has been internalized. A sublime subjectivity is made evident by the
form of the sentence. Not "O magnify with me," but "My soul doth
magnify." It is my whole being that magnifies.

II. THE SOUL

The Hebraic notion of *nephesh*, commonly translated "soul,"
does not correspond to the Greek idea of *psychê*, which in turn, during
Hellenistic times, implied a dualistic anthropology, or dichotomy between body and soul. Western mentality has been warped by this time-
honored mistranslation.

In Hebrew thought-form there is no distinction between those
two elements of the human personality, one of which would be pure
and immortal ("the soul") and the other corrupt and terminated in
death ("the flesh"). The Hebrew *nephesh* is approximately a synonym
of the Hebrew *basar*, "flesh." The only nuance between the two
words is dictated by contextual usage: *nephesh* stresses the idiosyncracy
of an individual and also the totality of being, in a single person,
whereas *basar* tends to emphasize the commonality of the human race.
Thus, the soul is just as carnal as the flesh, if one may so express it.
In contemporary culture, Hebraic anthropology of oneness is being

Prayerful Woman

revived by the use of the composite word "psychosomatic," which, precisely for want of an English equivalent, brings together the Greek word *psyche*, "soul," with the Greek word *sôma*, "body."

An accurate but admittedly drab rendering of the first line might be,

> My whole being, body and soul, celebrates the greatness of
> the Lord.

Indeed, since the Magnificat was composed directly in honor of Mary, the expectant mother, one might state without irreverence that the singer is affirming in her own flesh the thrill of spirituality. She ascribes the mystery of her motherhood to the "greatness of the Lord."

III. THE NAME

The divine name evokes the paradox of Israel's faith in its entirety. The name "the Lord" corresponds to the Greek *ho Kyrios*, with which the Jewish translators of the Hebrew scripture used to render the ineffable Hebrew name of the Deity, *Yahweh*.[1]

On the one hand, God is God because he has intervened in the tragic enslavement of the Hebrews in Egypt, and he has reversed the normal course of history. Yahweh is God because he is different from all "gods," which are projections of human interpretations of natural forces, especially those of fertility.

Yahweh is God, different from all gods of the nations, because his name means "He-Who-Causes-To-Be," the third person masculine singular of the causative mode of the verb *hawah*—that is, *Yahweh*. The traditional translation "I am that I am" arose from the Jewish vocalization, in Hellenistic times of the famous sentence, "I cause to be whatever or whomever I cause to be" (Exod 3:14). Greek-speaking Jews made the phrase sound like a philosophical statement of ontology.

---

[1] The tetragrammaton "YHWH" was in early days most probably pronounced "Yahweh." The pronunciation "Jehovah" represents a Christian, medieval error which read together the sacred consonants with the vowels of the word "Adonay": "the Lord." This word was substituted in synagogal reading so that the name be not taken in vain.

The Greek translation of the Septuagint, which reflects the intellectual syncretism of Jews in Antioch, Alexandria, and even Jerusalem, rendered the phrase, *Egô eimi ho ôn,* "I am, even I, the Being!" Perhaps they wished to show their university colleagues that their religious traditions implied an ontological thinking similar to those of the philosophical schools of their cultural environment.

The name Yahweh, however, suggested to ancient Israel and early Judaism the notion of absolute sovereignty over the cosmos and within the history of humankind. The memory of the deliverance was the ground of Hebrew faith. Salvation meant originally liberation from economic and political slavery. The creed of Israel rested on the exodus:

> I am Yahweh who has delivered thee from the house of
> slaves.

At the same time, Yahweh is God because he also acts in secret through the character of simple human beings, even when he appears to be absent, or at least silent, perhaps even impotent, as at the time of the ruin of Jerusalem by Nebuchadnezzar of Babylon (sixth century), during the persecutions by the Persians (fifth century), the Seleucids (second century), and the Romans (first centuries B.C. and A.D.). For Jews inspired by the great prophets, piety was not corrupted by worldliness, escape from the political and economic imperialism of foreigners was only the prerequisite of true deliverance, which is salvation from enslavement to hate and the spirit of self-interest and revenge. Salvation for those thinkers of the prophetic tradition meant more than a new exodus implemented by a political Messiah. For the great prophets, the psalmists and the sages, however, Yahweh is God because he saves men and women from pride and self-aggrandizement. The early Christians were Jews who were severed from political Judaism and who transformed the Passover, the feast of political liberation, into Easter, the feast of spiritual liberation and of new life.

This is precisely the theme which the poet of the Magnificat expounds in the second half of the first distich,

And my spirit is thrilled within God, my salvation (vs 46*b*).

IV. THE SPIRIT

A subtle step has been taken from the first stich to the second. The Magnificat had begun with a musical and perhaps choreographic act. The whole being of Mary extols the greatness of Yahweh as the sovereign of nature and history. A theological heir to the early Yahwist faith, she is presented as the singer of the magnalia Dei, grand opera of time.

The entire poem opens with the theme which will be developed throughout its subsequent lines: true freedom. This is the reason for which exegetes, and musicians who composed settings for the liturgy of Vespers, understood the first stich as a celebration, not of Mary alone, but of the whole church of God.

In the Magnificat, Mary shows herself to be the first daughter of the church. Composers, for this opening line, generally employ a full chorus, because Mary is the collective symbol of the entire family of humankind. But the mood swiftly passes from the universal and the corporate to the personal, the subjective, the intimate, the secret, "And my spirit is thrilled with God, my salvation."

Musicians, some of whom have revealed themselves as the shrewdest of exegetes and the boldest of theologians, prefer to use, after the full chorus of the first stich, a single soprano voice for the second stich. Revolutionary religion, the religion which creates a trend for centuries thereafter, labors at first in solitariness. Only afterwards does it open a vista hitherto hidden from society and command the media of diffusion. Mary is now confiding her secret to her kinswoman, Elizabeth. She is a prophet daring to share her most intimate jewel: my spirit thrills!

The word *spirit*, like the word *soul*, does not designate a distinctive part of the human personality, different from the flesh or from the mind. It points to that particular faculty of human beingness in its totality which is attuned to the intimations of infinity. At first, the word *ruach*, in Greek *pneuma*, was applied to strange powers ascribed to the influence of a deity, a *daimon* (beneficent or malevolent), or a "spirit." Until Ezekiel, in the sixth century B.C., the great prophets generally

avoided its use for describing their "in-*spir*-ation," because it migh
have led to a confusion between them and Canaanite diviners. They
dissociated themselves from the ecstatic dancers and madmen whom
Saul had met on the road after having been anointed by the prophet
Samuel in the tenth century. Two hundred years later, the prophet
Hosea quoted his enemies mocking him and calling him, the man of
the spirit, "a fool" (Hos 9:7).

The spirit was a force comparable to a tempest, which overwhelmed even the deep. The spirit of Yahweh jumped and skipped
over Samson, a shady character at best (Judg 14:6). It became an apt
vehicle for describing the element of the irrational in religious trance.
The wise men may have sought to rescue its positive significance when
they depicted the spirit of Elohim as fluttering like a mother bird over
her brood at creation (Gen 1:2). The femininity of the divine spirit
(*ruach* is a feminine word) was lost to the western world because the
Greek *pneuma* and the Latin *spiritus* are of the neuter and masculine
genders, respectively. Milton was the victim of this misapprehension
when he compared the spirit to the masculine agent of creation in his
famous apostrophe,

> . . . Thou, O Spirit . . .
> Dovelike sat'st brooding on the vast Abyss,
> And mad'st it pregnant.[2]

In early Christianity the word was applied to the phenomena of
glossolalia. St. Paul cautioned against the gift of spiritual possession.
By the time of the editing of the book of Acts, the gift of the Spirit on
the day of Pentecost was presented as xenoglossia, the speaking in
actual foreign tongues, rather than glossolalia, the so-called charismatic
gift of heavenly speech. Nevertheless, the apostles must have looked
somewhat enraptured, since outsiders thought them to be intoxicated
with wine.

The singer of the Magnificat did not refer to the Holy Spirit, but
she applied the term "spirit" to herself, as her faculty of exultation. In

---

[2] *Paradise Lost*, Bk. 1, 11. 17–21.

: of the Magnificat, hearers or readers could not miss
tween "my spirit" and the secret awareness of the
n. Gabriel had said to Mary, "The Holy Spirit shall
.... upon thee, and the power of the Most High shall overshadow
thee" (Lk 1:35). The allusion was not to a myth of sexual encounter
between a god and a woman, typical of ancient Near Eastern and
Greek religions, but it referred plainly to the Hebrew motif of the
"deep-darkness" (*'araphel*), which concealed the presence of Yahweh
on the holy mountain (Exod 20:18) and in the temple of Jerusalem
(I Kgs 8:12).

V. THE THRILL

In the Magnificat, the "spirit" is that aspect of the human personality which may be attuned to the divine Spirit, but it is not to be
separated from the notion of bodily oneness already expressed by the
concept of the soul. Consequently, the verb "thrills," which renders
the Greek *egalliasen* and the Hebrew *taggel*, "exults," designates the
delight which includes the whole spectrum of hedonic sensation or
pleasurable feeling.

Cognates in the other Semitic languages suggest that the Hebrew
word *gîl*, through one of its verbal voices, *gilgal*, refers to spiritual
dances around the vernal tree, which in northern latitudes have given
rise to the folklore of the maypole. In Arabic the cognate verb means
in one of its voices "to exult" and in another "to shriek in mystical
rapture," or again, "to emit a primal scream." In some erotic poems it
alludes to orgasmic ecstasy.

The poet of the Magnificat, however, was nurtured in the termi-
nology of the Hebrew scripture. The first and second lines of the hymn
strikingly echo the song of Hannah, Samuel's mother, who had been
saved from sterility.

> My heart rejoices in the Lord . . .
> I delight in thy salvation (1 Sam 2:1).

Similarly, the psalmist who has just escaped deathly trials sings,

> My soul shall thrill in the Lord;
> It will delight in his salvation (Ps 35:9 [Gr. 34:9]).

Overcoming the fear of destitution and perhaps of extinction, the prophet Habakkuk exclaims,

> Yet will I rejoice in the Lord!
> Let me thrill in the God of my salvation (Hab 3:18).

Such traditional phrases were made almost trite by devotional repetition in the course of the ages, but the Magnificat gives them new sparkle in a succinct and more effective expression of exaltation. Unlike Hannah, or the psalmist, or the prophet, who had faced the hostility of enemies, the sarcasm of envious rivals or the specter of starvation, Mary did not have to deal with the scorn of other women, the hatred of adversaries, or the dread of a worldwide winter, but she had a secret, and she looked upon her incredible elation against the broad canvas of pain amongst the whole humankind. And thus she could sing,

> My spirit is thrilled in the God of my salvation.

The context of the sentence shows that the poet was not a sectarian seeking to escape from the tragedies of history. Similarly, the singer was not a victim of glossolalia, nor the subject of a pantheistic identification with an infinite nature. Her spirit exults *within* God. She is surrounded by the reality of the divine. Embraced by the Lord of the cosmos, she is not deluded into divinity. The distinction between object and subject is maintained throughout her expostulation. Communion is union, not fusion, even less assimilation or identification.

Salvation through the intervention of God is far more than deliverance from enmity or destitution. Within the total context of scripture, the themes of the exodus, of the conquest of the land, even the land of promise, are now superseded by human renewal independent of geography or race. Salvation is presence transmuting outward defeat into inward triumph.

Biblical theology, viewed as a historical vortex of conflicting forces within twelve centuries of hopes, massacres, military victories, and political corruption, is the repeatedly revised paradigm of divine presence, even and especially when that presence remains elusive, and escapes human possessiveness. The person of Jesus, born in poverty and later executed with common thieves by a world empire, became the live Lord of the earliest church. The singer looked backwards to the annunciation of his birth as an unknown infant carried in an unknown mother's womb. Presence is manifested in absence, or at least in silence and in seeming impotence.[3]

To stress the magnalia Dei through the exodus and the conquest of the land and to extol God through wonders in nature or history, as traditional Judaism and conventional Christianity have done, is to miss the other side of Yahweh's disclosure to his own—Jeremiah, Job, Second Isaiah, the authors of Pss 51, 73, 139, and other poets. Martin Buber well saw that in the discourses from the whirlwind in the Joban masterpiece, which precisely argued against the simplistic idea of retributive justice, for peoples and for individuals, God offered Job no other answer to his questions than the gift of himself.

In spite of the caution with which Jesus refused to ascribe sudden misfortune to sinfulness, many conservative Jews and Christians still hold to the Deuteronomic dogma of rewards and punishments. The Magnificat, on the contrary, discerned the subtle and higher meaning of inner salvation.

VI. THE WOMAN-SLAVE

The second half of the first strophe refers directly to the response Mary made to the angel's announcement,

> For he has regarded the low estate of his woman-slave
> (vs 48*a*).

The word "humility" stands for the Greek *tapeinôsis*, which the Septuagint almost always used for the Hebrew *'oni.* It designates "ex-

---

[3] See Samuel Terrien, *The Elusive Presence: The Heart of Biblical Theology* (San Francisco: Harper & Row, 1984), pp.265 ff., 361 ff., 476.

treme want" or even "destitution," such as that of the Hebrew slaves in the concentration camps of the Pharaoh. It implies also a condition of responsiveness, of open receptivity, which in turn may be the result of existential extremity, but in fact represents the triumph of faith over fate.

Once again, the singer evokes the liberation of the whole being, a deliverance from inner evil as well as from outer tyranny, the shedding of selfishness and even the freedom from the fear of death.

A close link joins this sentence to the preceding one. Biblical theology seeks to discern the continuity of the stream, from the call of Abraham to the cross of Jesus. It thus discovers already in the exodus good news of grace before and above a rigid code of prohibitions and obligations. The Pentateuch is gospel rather than law. The word Torah, in any case, originally meant "story of nurture and of growth" before it meant "instruction" and eventually "law." Its root is akin to the words for teacher and for autumn rain, when greenness is revived after the death of nature in summer heat. This is the reason for which Christians should amend the traditional opposition between "law" and "gospel" and consider the Old Testament, like the New, not as a burden of duty but as an offer of life.

William Blake's designation of the Bible as "The Great Code of Art" should be purified of its legalistic distortions. In the Magnificat, Mary is a woman-slave of God, but her response to the angel is not an obedience of fear but a response of love. She makes herself available to grace. She is a vessel open to the future.

The word *shiphchah*, "woman-slave," is derived from a root which still carries among nomadic Arabs overtones or undertones of elemental life in the desert. The verb from which the noun is formed means "to pour" and alludes to the basic realities of daily existence: to pour, from a spring or a cistern, the water of survival; to shed blood, the substance of life, applicable to woman in her femininity or to a man whenever a raid threatens the security of the tribal group; and finally, to ejaculate sperm in the act of procreation.

Although popular etymology is not recognized by modern linguists as a tool of semantics, it has played an important and sometimes humorous part in the shaping of epic narratives. For example, the traditions of Genesis spoke of Jacob as "a supplanter," from his name *Ya'aqob*, literally, "he who kicks the heel," and of *Israel* as "he who wrestles with God." Etymological connotations, whether scientifically correct or not, are still remembered by modern Beduin, whose art of story-telling is scintillating with etymological fantasy.

VII. HAPPINESS

The poet of the Magnificat may or may not have been conscious of the semantic connotations of the word for female slave, but surely the phrase of the third stich in the first strophe brought out dramatically the contrast between Mary's confession of unworthiness and the magnitude of her destiny. In its context, the woman-slave of the Lord is presented as the very symbol of the *telos*—end and purpose of history—at the same time as she was the first daughter of the church.

Therefore, a new anticipation of the goal of history brings the first strophe to a climax:

Thus, on account of this, behold, all generations shall celebrate my happiness (vs 48*b*).

Mary is the mouthpiece of the future family of God. She is the vanguard of the *ecclesia*—when the word "church" meant simply "assembly."

Happiness means responsibility. It must spread to others and conquer the ravages of the decaying past, always renewing the present into the future. Translated from the highly probable reconstitution of the Hebrew original, this line discloses the unexpected power of a contained emotion.

Literally, the sentence might be rendered, "All generations will at once acknowledge and sing the ongoingness of my well-being." Mary is the first daughter of the church, for the call she has received, her *klesis*, flowers into the *ekklesia*—the assembly of the new people of God.

Mary is the first daughter of the church, for her vocation (*klesis*) includes all generations of those who will form after her the *ekklesia*.

The translated phrase "will be blessed," or more accurately, "will proclaim my happiness," stands in Hebrew as a single word, *ye-ash-sherûni*. The proto-Semitic root of the verb means "will go forward," or, in the intensive-causative voice, "will earnestly wish me to walk on the way."

What is the significance of happiness in Hebrew-Christian dynamics? To be happy is to race toward a goal, to look ahead, and also to lead others. Happiness is purposeful—a becoming movement—and it eventually must be growing within the collectivity. Neither egocentric nor individualistic nor merely hedonistic, but eudemonic in the social sense. It is catching and spreading.

Literally, the sentence might be rendered, "All generations will at once acknowledge and sing the ongoingness of my well-being." Mary is the first daughter of the church, for the call she has received, her *klesis*, flowers into the *ekklesia*—the assembly of the new people of God.

Mary is the first daughter of the church, for her vocation (*klesis*) includes all generations of those who will form after her the *ekklesia*. The translated phrase "will be blessed," or more accurately, "will proclaim my happiness," stands in Hebrew as a single word, *ye-ash-sher-ûni*. The proto-Semitic root of the verb means "will go forward," or, in the intensive-causative voice, "will earnestly wish me to walk on the way."

What is the significance of happiness in Hebrew-Christian dynamics? To be happy is to race toward a goal, to look ahead, and also to lead others. Happiness is purposeful—a becoming movement—and it eventually must be growing within the collectivity. Neither egocentric nor individualistic nor merely hedonistic, but eudemonic in the social sense. It is catching and spreading.

Obviously, the traditional rendering "blessed" is inadequate, for its meaning is inevitably static. Besides, the Hebrew language clearly distinguishes between the idea of dynamic happiness, *ashrê*, literally, an exclamation of wish, "Oh the ongoing way of . . . ," and that of "being blessed" (*barûk*). These two concepts are somewhat synonymous but should not be confused. The first belongs to the vocabulary of the sages and of the wisdom-inspired psalmists. The second refers to the sacerdotal act of benediction by the priests. The first is an exhortation to take an existential risk. The second is a description of a state of being that results from the reception of a ritual gesture. "Blessed" is a passive participle in Hebrew as in English.

The Hebrew notion of happiness is a summons to the voyage of life from a leader. There is no doubt that Jesus borrowed the sapiential term *ashrê* rather than its priestly equivalent *barûk* in a series of misnamed "beatitudes." The Latin *beatus*, from which the word "beatitude" arises, is not satisfying, since its cognate "beatific" suggests the image of a saint whose statue is immobile in a niche.

The Greek-speaking Jews of Alexandria and Antioch who, in Hellenistic times, translated the scripture into Greek, attempted to discover a Greek rendering for the Hebrew idiom *ashrê*, "Oh the happiness of . . . ," but the best they could do was to select the word *makarios*, which in Homer or in classical Greek described the repose of the shades in the eternal twilight of Elysian Fields. We still say, pointedly, "the blessed dead."

The Magnificat does not concern itself with a peaceful Hades. Mary sings, "Behold, on account of the secret manifestation of God which the coming birth of my infant will display to the centuries ahead, all generations will sing my happiness."

The Magnificat, a hymn of the early Jerusalem church, celebrates the certainty that a simple man, a single man, rejected of men, would suffer the ignominy and the death of a slave and yet explode the idea of Israel—the slave of Yahweh—into a new, inclusive, and even universal peoplehood. His mother, the woman-slave of Yahweh, invites future humanity to participate in her happiness. Men and women of tomorrow, for ages to come, will step forward into the unknown and will blaze a trail into no-man's-land, for they will be motivated and activated by a vision of "the union of opposites" and the reconciliation of antagonists. That historical Christendom has in many respects failed to fulfill its mission does not in any way deter from the certainty which animated the early community. This solid faith, from century to century, has fired the foresight and heroism of reformers.

The first strophe of the Magnificat issues a solemn order to Christians, that they proclaim Mary's happiness in their act of worship and in their earthly life. They will make that happiness real within time.

They will prolong, continue, broaden, and incarnate Mary's expectation. They will be happy only insofar as they fulfill that hope.

At this state of the hymn, however, the voice remains, not still, but reserved, for it is restricted to the visitation scene, when two expectant mothers exchange their most intimate secrets. A modern poet has expressed the mood:

ME DICENT BEATAM OMNES GENERATIONES
So small a thing, so slim a wedge
Of time, to be the container of
Such wordless happiness, such stark
Awareness of the moment's grave
Translucency. The very edge
Of winter melted, and was love,
And gave, against the lonely dark
An amber time of touch to save.[4]

VIII. MUSICAL ILLUSTRATIONS

Strophe I
[Latin Version]

46. *Magnificat anima mea Dominum:*
47. *Et exultavit spiritus meus in Deo salutari meo.*
48. *Quia respexit humilitatem ancillae suae:*
     Ecce enim ex hoc beatam me dicent omnes generationes.

A poem is modulated speech. It is music with words, not words with music. This is one of the reasons why its interpretation requires far more than verbal analysis. The elucidation of its key words and the

---

[4] Bonny Elizabeth Parker, "An Amber Time," *The Christian Science Monitor*, March 30, 1963. Reprinted by permission from *The Christian Science Monitor*, ©1963 The Christian Science Publishing Society. All rights reserved.

examination of its structure and of its thematic articulations have their legitimate and indispensable place. Such a study may even be a help for the hearing of the Magnificat in music. At the same time, scholarly exegesis lacks the mode of instant communication which singing, with or without orchestral accompaniment, provides as it entices the attuned ear.

For centuries, the chanting of the Magnificat and of the other canticles of the nativity was carried out with various alterations, adaptations, and inventions from the pre-Christian Greek modes and also from the melodies of the synagogue. In the course of time, chanting styles changed from Ambrosian to Byzantine and eventually to Gregorian. Named not altogether correctly after Gregory I (590–604), the Gregorian passed through several phases of development in the Carolingian, Romanesque, and Gothic ages and dominated a large section of the western church as plainsong, at least until the third quarter of the twentieth century.

When minstrels accompanied the troubadours and secular music became polyphonic, the church attempted to maintain the strict use of Gregorian chant. Male monastics and parish priests sang the Psalms and the mass *a capella* as impersonally and abstractly as humanly possible. Little by little, the hierarchy tolerated polyphonic music with instrumental accompaniment. During the fourteenth century, in an age intermittently plagued by the Black Death and a multitude of military disasters, the people wanted pleasure and artistic imagination, even in the sanctuary. It was also the time when religious drama flourished before the portals of cathedrals. The mystery plays celebrated Adam and Eve, Job, the nativity, and the passion. Under the influence of the theater, communal worship tended to personalize the grand opera of the Christian year, from Advent to All Hallows. The objective timelessness of the Opus Dei which had been brought out by Gregorian chant was gradually displaced by subjective and emotional expressionism. The Ars Nova invaded church music precisely when the subtlety of dramatization which Gregorian chant had portrayed seemed to have become inaccessible to untutored ears.

1. *Johannes de Quatris* (ca. 1335–1400) was a priest living in Paris. A younger contemporary of Guillaume de Machaut (1300–

1377), he composed a Magnificat which is the first-known Ars Nova setting for the song of Mary. Its earliest surviving manuscript[5] is dated 1436. In polyphonic proto-motet form, it constitutes a transition from chanted reading to modulated and orchestrated interpretation of the words. The musical exegesis of the Magnificat was born.

In the recorded example, the polyphonic instrumentation of the long prelude that introduces the song itself probably represents the decisions of musicologists.[6]

The first line, *Magnificat anima mea Dominum*, was not included in the manuscript score, for it was still intoned in plainsong *a cappella* by the celebrant. The second line, *Et exultavit spiritus meus in Deo salutari meo*, was given a fully expressive range for two soprano voices. It produces the effect of an intimate dialogue between Mary's soul and her spirit. Praise of God's greatness is rapturously but soberly allied to the thrill of the mother-to-be. Solemnity in the face of transcendence is balanced by delicacy and reticence.

2. *William Byrd* (1543–1623) was a brilliant pupil of Thomas Tallis (1505–1585), who himself wrote several settings for the Magnificat. Byrd was appointed organist of the Lincoln Cathedral at the age of twenty and soon joined his master at the Chapel Royal in London. Although he was a Roman Catholic, he remained under the protection of Queen Elizabeth. He composed both Roman masses and Anglican liturgies. Four of his settings of the Magnificat are known, some to be sung in Latin, others in English.

Byrd's *Magnificat* for "The Great Service" provides a balanced treatment, which stands halfway between the medieval objectivity of the Latin liturgy and the ethereality of the Anglican chant. He has bequeathed to the Church of England and her offshoots across the world a model of Mary's hymn as is used at Evensong.

---

[5] Oxford, Bodleian, Can. Misc. 213, dated 1436, "in the month of May, in Venice."

[6] The Ensemble Polyphonique de la Radio et Télévision Française, which recorded the piece (Inédits RTF, No. 955010), used reed flutes, cromorne, Poitevin oboe, rebec, vielle, musette, psalterion and shawm. The same musical phrase is repeated seven times with subtle variations of instrumental sequences.

The *Magnificat* for "The Great Service" reaches a level of de-
nuded adoration at the price, as in the plainsong, of a relative staticity
of mood quite alien to the ongoingness of the Hebrew poem. In the
opening lines, Mary's dual voices are not down-to-earth. The counterpoint is dense. Chords suggest a dedicated and even light humility.
They convey the innocence and the hope of the maiden "full of
grace."

3. *Georg Philipp Telemann* (1681–1767) presents a contrast of
flamboyance with the chaste style of the Elizabethan composer, but in
his interpretation of Mary's hymn, he is not devoid of inwardness. His
Grand Magnificat in G Major may not appeal to everyone. From the
Renaissance, still closely linked with medieval forms of worship, to
the High German Lutheran Baroque, influenced by the spectacular
orchestration of the Italianate triumphalism, the change is consider-
able. German Lutherans could be as exuberant in Hamburg and Bre-
men as Venetian Roman Catholics in the Basilica of San Marco.

Contemporary of Händel, Rameau, Vivaldi, Domenico Scarlatti,
and Johann Sebastian Bach, Telemann reflects in his *Grand Magnificat in G Major* the fashionable styles of Italy, France, and Poland,
starkly adapted to the German taste of the period. Successively Kapell-
meister at the courts of Sornau and Eisenach, later on at churches in
Frankfurt and Hamburg, he represents a Lutheran grandeur that is in
some ways comparable to the grandiosity of post-Tridentine Roman
Catholicism.

The instrumental prelude, with fanfares and drums proper for
military tunes, pictures a festive and exuberant church symbolized by
Mary. She throws around the lush flowers of her offering in praise of
the divine Benefactor. The motif of the majesty of God the most high
reappears in the core-verse with an explosive *Fecit potentiam* (vs 51),
whose brio was prone to please princes and burghers. The whole *Magnificat* is then bound with the Gloria in a final appearance of the same
motif for an almost riotous celebration of the Advent and Christmas
holy days.

At the same time, an alto solo delineates *Quia respexit humilitatem ancillae suae* with genuine penetration into the psyche of a

woman who willingly responds to her unexpected and increasing mission.

4. *Johann Sebastian Bach* (1685–1750). The Leipzig genius is probably the greatest exponent of Lutheran theology through music. His oratorios and cantatas show an original and daring understanding of Hebrew-Christian dynamics, not only by his selections of Old Testament passages paired with New Testament parallels but also by the precise sequence in which they are juxtaposed for cumulative effect. The *Magnificat in D* (1723) shows the master exegete's talent for sensing in the lines of the text the correspondences between the Hebrew hopes and their Christian acceptance.

The entire setting is preceded by an instrumental Symphonia, which, at times, with blaring silver trumpets, is punctuated by muffled and sparse percussion. Bach adumbrates in the symphonic introduction an anticipated triumph at the end of history. He seemingly brings together heaven and earth, embraced in *Heilsgeschichte* (history of salvation). Through the device of poetic inclusion, the motif of the Symphonia reappears briefly in the Gloria at the end of the work.

The first line, *Magnificat anima mea Dominum*, is sung by a full chorus, for it belongs to the whole church—past, present, and future. Supported yet never overwhelmed by an orchestra of strings, three flutes, two oboes, three silver trumpets, tympani, harpsichord, and organ, the five-voiced chorus accelerates its tempo. The amplitude swells to a fortissimo as if the assurance of attaining a this-worldly happiness and an other-worldly end has seized even the entire assembly of the saints.

In contrast, the *Et exultavit spiritus meus*, written for a second soprano, floats above a counterpoint of strings. It blends purity with tenderness, but it becomes tinged with foreboding. The sunny sky is clouded, and the darkness has not yet arrived but it can be guessed at, for the duet of the voice with an oboe d'amore leaves no doubt as to the eventuality of death.

This somber mood is not final. It is suddenly swept away in a repetition by full chorus and orchestra of ninety-six antiphonal expostulations of *Omnes generationes*. The happiness of Mary and the ongoingness of the church, of which she is the first daughter, involves blasts of trumpets. These do not all sound like the sharp call of the last judgment: they are a veritable apotheosis of jubiliation.

5. *Alan Hovhaness* (b. 1911). The marriage of moods between exultation and anticipation of sorrow permeates the setting of the Magnificat by Hovhaness, an American-born Armenian, who breaks with the Baroque and Romantic traditions of the west. His work is pervaded by Greek, Byzantine, and Armenian modes, and a particular brand of mysticism at once sharpens and tames his boldness. The *Celestial Fanfare* starts with an evocation of tuning for the heavenly instruments and of humming for the angelic voices. It then grows into a bassoon elegy that evolves into a serene meditation. The whole church, first of women, then of men, follows in chorus.

The *Et exultavit spiritus meus* becomes the responsibility of the tenor voice—a tender expression of inner joy—punctuated by a series of pizzicato string ornaments. In the *Quia respexit humilitatem ancillae suae*, a female voice gives unabashed and sometimes heart-rending inflections to Mary's adolescent purity, surprise, and final acceptance of a life which will be full of tribulation. The woman-slave of the Lord follows her goal with a steady determination, but even before the birth of the holy infant she prefigures the *Mater Dolorosa*.

Chapter 3

The Compassion of God

49. For he that is mighty hath done to me great things;
    And holy is his name.

50. And his mercy is on them that fear him
    From generation to generation.

The second strophe (vss 49–50) is articulated directly out of the first strophe. As in Greek or Latin, the expression "great things" corresponds in Hebrew (see Table II) to the opening word, "Magnificat." The poet elaborates on the double motif which was already hinted at in the first strophe. Mary casts a historical glance backward to the exodus, and a psychological insight forward, to the incarnation.

I. TO ME

The personal pronoun "to me" interiorizes the theology of salvation. Liberation from political tyranny and economic slavery means little unless it be also deliverance from self and from egocentricity of clan, class, nation, race, or any other closed group, including synagogue and church.

A grateful acknowledgement of the *Magnalia Dei* in history forms the basis of the Hebraic confession of faith and the preface to the decalogue:

> I am Yahweh thy God,
> Who has brought thee out of the land of Egypt,
> Away from the house of slaves (Exod 20:2).

Total allegiance to such a sovereign Lord was vitiated ever since the Sinai event by the corruption of chieftains, princes, and people. The covenant carried with its promise the risk of annulment (Exod 19:4–6). Courageously, the prophet Jeremiah declared that it was null and void and that a new covenant would be sealed only after a new creation, when the law would be written upon human hearts (Jer 31:31–33).

When the Magnificat is viewed within the context of the Lukan gospel of the nativity, it hails not a new covenant within this economy of historical existence, but a new covenant in the world to come. The wondrous conception of an infant in the womb of a simple servant of the Lord is the sign of a new creation. God alone shows his nobility by transferring the notion of power over the cosmos and history into the notion of power within the human character.

Just as faith of the fathers recognized the wonders of the spirit of God brooding over the deep, so also the faith of Mary greets the creation of the new being. The early church used the language of myth to convey this mystery. To be born again and to live again is the cardinal hope of the apostle Paul. The center of that good news which set the Roman world afire was the assurance of participation in the new being, not only at the end of history but already now, in some incipient stirring of the *kainê ktisis*—the new creation (Gal 6:15). The "great things" which the Lord has wrought for Mary are the tokens of the new economy of life upon this earth.

Through the device of rhetorical juxtaposition, the Lukan editor of stories and hymns surrounding the birth of Jesus proposed an understanding of the *magna* ("great things") as the wonder of the annunciation. He did so in full awareness of the strange language which the mythical narrative lends to the angel Gabriel's intervention. A myth is not a false report. As in the ancient meaning of *muthos*, it should be construed to be a story that carries a truth beyond the limited possibilities of rational knowledge. There are dead myths, and also live myths.

Young Girl

The angel Gabriel greets Mary with the words, "The Lord be with thee!" This is far more than a casual salutation. Mary is addressed in the same way as were the patriarchs and the judges when they were called upon to deliver Israel from oppression. She is thereby associated with the great prophets summoned to pronounce the doom of kings, princes, priests, and people unwilling to mend their ways. Moreover, this salutation is preceded by a peculiar formula:

Hail! Mary, Thou, the One Being Graced!

II. GRACE AS LONGING

The verb used here is borrowed from the language of divine forgiveness. In Hebrew, *chen*, "grace," is derived from the verb *chanan*, "to have mercy," which in pre-Elizabethan English was rendered "to grace [someone]." It describes the longing of God for humanity. It is a word carrying the image of a mother always pining for the fruit of her womb. To God is ascribed a maternal emotion, as in the first line of Psalm 51 that has given the liturgical prayer of the eucharist, *Kyrie eleison!* Far more than "Lord, have mercy!" which suggests pardon for prisoners, it implies an inner turmoil within the divine reality, since the psalmist continues thus:

According to the multitude of thy motherly compassions!

Quite rightly, the earlier English versions depicted the love of God as "bowels of mercy." Like the psalmist, Mary is the object of God's longing. This is the meaning of the Hebrew concept of grace.

As it has been pointed out above, the Spirit of God—a word in the feminine gender—was brooding like a mother bird over the primeval waters and it transformed the deep into an inhabitable earth. Its presence was then sensed as the "thick darkness" that covered Mount Sinai and became linked, centuries later, to the total obscurity which filled the innermost room of the Jerusalem temple (I Kgs 8:12). In the Lukan gospel of the nativity the two themes have become interwoven. "The Holy Spirit shall come upon thee, and the power of the Most High shall overshadow thee!" (Lk 1:35). The power that creates a new being in history is moved by the compassions of the divine womb. The dialogue between the angel and Mary brings together the vision of a world a-forming, the memory of a people a-borning at Mt. Sinai, the motif of the presence hidden on Mt. Zion, and a still deeper marvel— the birth of the infant. The Magnificat miniatures and interiorizes the *magnalia Dei* in the *magna* done to a humble slave-woman of the Lord.

In the first strophe, Mary sang of her feminine self, thrilled with God's joy. In the second strophe, she continues the same theme, but she now "magnifies" it by her singing of God's own selfhood. The greatness done unto her transforms her infant into the vessel of the new being, the Imago Dei, the mirror of the Most High, the first born of a new race, the pioneer of tomorrow.

The principle of rhetorical juxtaposition, which was common in the literature of ancient Hebraism and appears also in the gospels, amply justifies this interpretation. And the appellation of God in the first line of the second strophe clinches the argument. The Lord is called "The Potent One."

III. THE POTENT ONE

The Greek *ho dunatos* (vs 49), "the Mighty One," is used in the Septuagint Bible to render several Hebrew names for Yahweh, the most common of which is *Hag-Gibbôr*, "The Hero." God is the Noble Lord, whose nobility lies in his devotion to his vassals, indeed to those who pay allegiance to him. A "nobleman" (*nadib*) is someone who will defend his group to the extent of *nedabah*, the free-will offering of himself. Semitic ears did not miss the assonance between the name *Hag-gibbôr*, "The Hero," and the angel's name, Gabriel. Both names are derived from the verbal root G.B.R. The Potent One, who moves the sun and all the stars, is also the actor of this event, who procreates the new being. Divine power is invisible until it metamorphoses women and men. If the discipline of the biblical theology respects the canonical growth of the entire scripture, it cannot stop with the events of the exodus and of the conquest. The covenant is not just an alliance with a chosen race to the exclusion of others. It must include the vision of the great prophets, who called for a new covenant, at the end of history.

IV. THE HOLY ONE

Each motif unfolds into the next. At initial glance, the second line of the second strophe, "And holy is his name," appears to be a casual and pious cliché, an almost hackneyed quotation of an ancient hymn. But the poet knew the context of this quotation and he apparently surmised that the poetic habits of his audience would also be stirred by the surrounding words,

> [The Lord] sent his redemption to his people;
> He has commanded his covenant for ever:
> Holy and fearful is his name (Ps 111:9).

The mere mention of the holiness of the name brings to mind the fearful obligation of the Sinai covenant. A high ethical standard of private and public morality remains inseparable from the demands of the covenant (Exod 19:5–6).

The name is Yahweh ("He-who-causes-to-be"). It is disclosed to Moses at the burning bush (Exod 3:14). It does not point to the reality of God within a philosophical structure of reality. The name stands for a presence which inclines itself toward humanity and yet remains far beyond a human grasp of machination. It denies the validity of the kind of mysticism that amounts to a psychological form of magic or of the illusory technique to enlist for one's own benefit the deified forces of nature.

The poet employs the method of *inclusio oppositorum*. The Potent One is Yahweh, and his name is "The Holy One." The presence is elusive, for the divinity is unapproachable and inaccessible to human desire. The presence inspires dread, for the divine demands pierce the heart of humankind. Yet, the presence summons life in the womb of a woman.

The story of another Mosaic theophany clearly bears a polemical intent when it opposes a theology of the name to a theology of the glory. Priests in their shrines and with their rites claim that they see the glory. Moses, the prophet par excellence, is tempted by the mystical vision and asks, "I beseech thee, show me thy glory!" (Exod 33:18). But his request is rejected, as Yahweh answers,

> I will proclaim the name of Yahweh before thee,
> And I will be gracious to whom I will be gracious . . . (vs 19b).

In the same narrative, the name is made parallel to the goodness of God (vs 19a). In other words, the name stands for the outgoing purpose of God toward humankind. It is holy, for the covenant is "commanded for ever" (Ps 111:9).

The Potent One is the creator of new beingness in human life, but his graciousness is never subject to human command. We are unable to encompass the infinity of the divine reality. We cannot penetrate to the core of being. Like Moses, we are denied the vision of glory. We can only hear the word, which commands us to follow a high standard of responsibility, individual and social, private and public, embracing all men and women.

The name means the revelation of the will of God for me and for humankind. I am called to obey the word. When in the Lord's Prayer I am bidden to say, "Hallowed be thy name," I commit myself to the wish of Mary in the Magnificat. I become a descendant of the prophet Isaiah, who responded, "Here am I, send me!" (Isa 6:8c). To repeat the Lord's Prayer is an awesome act, for it involves one in totality.

When Mary sings, "For his name is The Holy One," she takes seriously the command and the demand, and she yields to the divine word. She does not ask for the vision of glory, which, in effect, would correspond to the desire to be God. Moses indulges in a quest for mystical identity with infinity. He must remain content with the knowledge of his vocation. The line between the human and the divine remains clear. Man and woman eat of the fruit of the tree of infinite knowledge. The Hebraic idiom "good and evil" does not mean literally the awareness of ethical standards, but rather, divine omniscience (Gen 3:4). Man and woman do not become God, but God may become human.

In the lively myth of the Hebrew scriptures, the name sojourns as a nomad by night (1 Kgs 8:12). When the singer of the Magnificat says, "And his name is The Holy One," she means, "Let his will be done, on earth as it is in heaven!" The poem, born in the earliest days of the church, echoes the same theology as that of the first Christian community in Jerusalem, delighting in the presence of the living Lord. Yet, the human tragedy lies at the heart of the rejoicing.

V. THE DIVINE WOMB

Biblical theology not only compels a dark view of human intentions and achievements but also promotes with alacrity a most optimistic view of divine volition.

> And his compassions last from generation to generation
> (vs 50*a*).

As we move from the second to the third line of the second strophe, there seems at first to be no distinct sequence of thought, until we examine the word *rachmim*, "compassions." The Greek *eleos* and its Latin equivalent *misericordia* render fairly well the Hebrew *rachmim*, which contains the whole pathos or passion of unrequited love. It implies the sorry spectacle of history with its vicious circle of human greed and pride, which eventually vitiates the highest human virtue.

The Hebraic traditions of Genesis and Exodus, together with the great prophets' stringent appraisal of Israel and Judah during the conquest and the monarchy, reflect a desperate anthropology and a hopeful theology. Such a paradoxical understanding of the human adventure has little in common with the vagaries of the Age of Enlightenment.

Throughout the thousand years of ancient Israel and of early Judaism, from the Late Bronze Age to the Roman Empire, the realities of peoplehood and covenant are threatened by the nightmare of individual as well as social corruption. The early church, with its internecine dissensions and eventually its male hierarchy, did not fare better than the Jewish society from which it emerged. The new covenant, anchored in the life of Jesus, was unrealized in the life of the church.

It remains to this day eschatological—the ultimate hope of both Jewry and Christendom—for the end of history. Human enterprise is doomed to eventual failure unless it be divinely oriented. Women as well as men wish to be the captains of their souls and the centers of the universe. Sin is hardly more than anthropocentricity, especially when religion is nothing but spiritual idolatry.

The nobility of God the hero resides in his self-abasement for the sake of creating the new being. In Latin, *misericordia* means the destitution of the heart. To modern ears the word may suggest open-heart surgery, and the metaphor is one of risk with hope. John Calvin's seal represented an open hand, the hand of God, holding on its palm a human heart burning with a shining flame. This is the implication of *misericordia*—a burning and an obstinate love.

In the Lukan Greek, the word *eleos*, as in the Septuagint, renders the Hebrew *rachmim*, a plural of majesty for the singular *rechem*, "uterus." It introduces the boldly anatomical image of the femininity of God. The *misericordia* of Yahweh is comparable to a bleeding womb. Who can dare to repeat, after centuries of Christian misunderstanding, that the Old Testament knows nothing but a tribal deity, male, avenging, the personification of the thunderbolt, a tyrannical Father image?

God is the *Gibbôr*, the Nobleman, the Hero par excellence, because he never gives up. Like a mother, as well as like a father, the creator will never abandon his children. The prophet Hosea, in the eighth century B.C., portrayed the God of Israel as a cuckold husband. God goes on and on, the butt of mockery.

VI. NOT AFRAID

The true and lively myth is not the parting of the sea at the exodus, but the *misericordia* of Yahweh. Yet, not all human beings will discern the pathos in God's love. It is perceptible only to those who fear him—*timentibus eum* (vs 50a).

The Hebraic notion of fear is quite different from the modern connotation. For us, fear seems to have only a negative significance. It is a psychological and physical reaction of defense against danger, poverty, disease, or death, especially death understood as annihilation.

Is it true that our ultimate source of safety is in that oft-quoted phrase, "the sturdy child of terror," and our survival is "the twin brother of annihilation"? For prehistoric man the answer was Yes. For prehistoric man's heir in the twentieth century A.D., fear may lurk beneath psychological consciousness, repressed as the very idea of death.

In *Murder in the Cathedral* T. S. Eliot portrayed a madly apprehensive crowd at Canterbury anticipating a foul deed—the execution of Thomas à Becket:

> . . . our hearts are torn from us, our brains unskinned
>   like the layers of an onion, our selves are lost lost
> In a final fear which none understands.[1]

Quite different is the fear experienced by the lover of God. Pre-Islamic Arabs had a proverb that said, "There is something lacking in love without fear." They did not mean the fear of pain, or sado-masochistic subjection. To the contrary, they had in mind the fear of not pleasing the beloved, the apprehensiveness that haunts in the prospect of falling short of the beloved's expectation.

And so also with the fear of God.

It is not only the fear of inadequacy before the *misericordia Dei*, the destitute heart of God, that the poet of the Magnificat had in mind. The fear of God is not the dread of his judgment, but, rather, of his self-giving compassion. Those who fear him have become again as little children. They know he will forgive.

A prosaic but precise rendering of the last two lines in the second strophe might be, "And his self-giving love, which means the oblation of his own self, lasts across the ages, from parents to children, for those who love him with the terror of displeasing him. They fear his love, not his anger."

---

[1] T.S. Eliot, *Murder in the Cathedral* (New York: Harcourt, Brace and Company, 1935), p. 20.

Biblical theology, in the second strophe of the Magnificat, rehearses the history of our faith, from the gospel of the exodus to the gospel of Calvary. It underlines the awareness of human failure in the face of God's expectations. It prefigures the road to the crucifixion.

The theme of ecstasy tempered by fear, which at the end of the first strophe does not prevent the prediction of happiness for all generations, persists in the second strophe. The mood of exultation, however, is subdued, because the singer, who incarnates the mother-to-be, at once remembers and anticipates. The reminiscence is that of the annunciation.

> Wings beating about the room;
> The terror of all terrors that I bore
> The Heavens in my womb.

The foreboding is muted into a question:

What is this flesh I purchased with my pains?[2]

VII. MUSICAL ILLUSTRATIONS

STROPHE II

49. *Quia fecit mihi magna qui potens est*
    Et sanctum nomen eius
50. *Et misericordia eius a progenie in progenies*
    Timentibus eum.

Almost every setting of the Misericordia shows that musicians, with perspicacity often greater than that of scholars, have understood the theology of pathos hidden in these lines.

1. *Marc-Antoine Charpentier* (1634–1704). Even at the court of Versailles in the middle of the seventeenth century as well as in the

---

[2] "The Mother of God," *The Collected Poems of W.B. Yeats* (New York: Macmillan, 1959), p. 244.

churches of Paris at that period, austerity of devotion prevailed beneath the glitter of liturgical pomp and the splendor of orchestral instrumentation. Marc-Antoine Charpentier had been dazzled by Italian musical opulence, but he had also been strongly impressed by the Saracen style, which conferred upon Spanish music its exotic and frequently tragic melancholy. His evocation of the broken-heartedness of God contrasts dramatically with the white marble, the blue drapes, and the gold ornaments in the Royal Chapel at the palace of Louis XIV.

2. *Antonio Vivaldi* (1678–1741). Composing for the basilica of San Marco in Venice, Vivaldi, despite the grand manner of the Baroque idiom, sensed the somber view of humanity which underlies the second strophe of the Magnificat. The initial beat is that of a seemingly unavoidable doom and it leaves no room for hope. Little by little, however, the bass accompaniment modifies its tempo so that the monotony of human misery is transformed into the airy and illuminated cadences of the divine passion. Human misery conduces to unrelieved boredom, but now it is slowly transformed into a *basso ostinato*, like a repetitive pattern dawning through the divine *misericordia*. God's own misery is being extended to humanity, and thus its growing insistence manifests itself in successive urgings. God never tires. His *misericordia* surges; it rises, it swells. Nevertheless, the beat of human turpitude continues, unrelenting, banal, as trivial as evil. "When you have seen one slum, you have seen them all," remarked a now-forgotten politician.

A few bars before the end, a chromatic descent increases the feeling of horror. It appears to be a Baroque device which other masters like Buxtehude and J. S. Bach used for the crucifixion theme. Most likely, the tuning systems of the time, which included the mean tone, produced the effect of agony through the resulting dissonances.

Then listen to the way in which the musician summons from above a new form of power, which at the end will overcome the obsessive rhythm of sinfulness. Divine passion turns and turns, equally obstinate, equally unyielding, like the ocean surf. At last the tempest desists.

The minor chord is relieved. The major ending, called the Picardy third (tierce de Picardie), was a standard practice from about 1500

and continued throughout the Baroque period. It opens a ray
shine, and the musical phrase concludes in proclamation. Yet, it is still
a celebration of reticence.

3. *Johann Sebastian Bach* (1685–1750). The *Misericordia* of the
master par excellence, with its Italianate inflections, belongs to the highest
moment of Baroque music. But it breaks musical traditions for the settings
of the *Magnificat* by treating the poetic theme as a love duet. While
Bach's predecessors and most of his successors assign to this movement a
full chorus, as if the unfailing loyalty of God across the generations of
history requires the broad medium of the human collectivity, we have
here an aria for contralto and tenor. It is reminiscent of the allegorical use
of the Song of Songs in medieval Mariology. It may also allude to the
dialogue of the annunciation between Gabriel and Mary.

The beat of dead-end futility is still present, but soon it is replaced
by a syncopated dance step—the Siciliano—mostly on the cello, at
times accentuated by a staccato from double bass, and occasionally
punctuated by muffled percussion. It suggests the image of vine ten-
drils entwining—a persistent motif in medieval illuminations and folklore love songs.

As for the *timentibus*, the composer's intent is unmistakable.
Bach was not afraid of fear, for he knew the meaning of that peculiar
fear that is born of love.

4. *Carl Philipp Emanuel Bach* (1717–1788). A closer disciple
of the Italianate style than his father, C. P. E. Bach presents a pattern
similar to that of Vivaldi. It might be viewed, at least in this movement,
as taking a retrogressive path toward the early Baroque. In the middle
of the eighteenth century, he introduces a sustained sentiment sometimes bordering on sentimentality. The circumlocutions of the vocal
adornment stress the ups and downs of divine pathos and contrast with
the restraint of his father's treatment of the same motif. Like Vivaldi,
he chooses a throbbing eighth note motif throughout, with recurrent
chromaticism and vivid word painting for *timentibus*. Suspensions in
female voices against the thrust of male voices on the beat create an
effect of trembling and, the next time, a similar effect through the
sequential use of appogiatura.

Icon of Mary

Chapter 4

The Mother of Revolution

CORE-VERSE

51. He hath shown strength with his arm;
     He hath scattered the proud in the imagination
     of their hearts.

STROPHE III

52. He hath put down the mighty from their seats,
     And exalted them of low degree.
53. He hath filled the hungry with good things;
     And the rich he hath sent empty away.

I. THE TRUE STRENGTH

The core-verse (vs 51) unites the themes of the incarnation and
of social justice. It links the restoration of justice within the human
family to the mystery of a birth.

"He hath shown strength" does not suggest a past tense in Hebrew. The Hebraic verb refers to the act of creation. It transcends
the categories of time which we have inherited from Greco-Roman
antiquity. The theme of divine power was initially hinted at in the first
strophe and then explicitly introduced in the second strophe with the
ascription of Mary's secret wonder to the "The Potent One" (vs 49a).
The divine hero, the noble God, appears now in full display. In the
Hebrew reconstitution of the poem, the correspondence of words
strikes the observer with the inescapable evidence: *Hag-Gibbôr* has

done *geburôt* (common verbal stem G.B.R.). "The Hero has acted out his heroic deed," or "The Potent One has shown his potency." In Latin, St. Jerome sensed an etymological and semantic Hebrew relationship which is not visible in the Greek. The line of the second strophe,

Quia fecit mihi magna qui potens est (vs 49*a*)

is sustained and amplified in the core-verse,

Fecit potentiam in brachio suo (vs 51*a*).

Once again, a singer of the poem in Hebrew could not miss seeing here an allusion to the name of the angel Gabriel, especially with the presence of the expression, "with his arm."

The word for "arm" (from *zara'*II) is probably used as a euphemistic equivalent of its homonym "seed," "sperm," "posterity" (from *zara'*I). In view of these associations of sounds and meanings, it is not inappropriate to suggest that the poet had in mind the early notion of the church as the posterity of the living Christ. Christians are associated with their God not only through their faith in the living Lord Jesus but also through their liturgical participation in the annunciation of his conception.

The secret growth of the child in his mother's womb amounts to a manifestation of strength disguised in humility and clothed in weakness.

The poet is no longer referring to the *magnalia Dei* in nature with the taming of tumultuous forces of evil like the sea, the discomfiture of Pharaoh's chariots and horsemen, or—antithetically—the theophany with fire descending upon the holy mountain. The thaumaturgical aspects of the national epic are relegated to a distant and terminated past. A new economy of history is inaugurated. God intervenes in the life of a humble woman to initiate a way of raising humankind to the level of true humanity. The marvel of annunciation is spelled out in the Magnificat as the wonder of human rebirth.

Inner vision as a response to the heroic deed of the hero-God becomes a source of human liberation. *Theoria* (vision) leads to *praxis* (action). The revolution is coming, but not in a Marxist sense. God is the doer. The fields of force move from the exodus, when God is present, to the Babylonian exile, when God is absent. They point to the cross of Golgotha, when God remains silent. The *Deus Absconditus* is the God who conceals himself in order to become, in a new manner, the *Deus Revelatus*. He reveals himself in the womb of a woman.

Some wit has remarked that, at the Council of Trent, the Virgin Mary lost her sovereignty of Heaven by one vote. One may add, in utmost reverence, that the Magnificat presents her as the first daughter of the church and as the mother of revolution.

II. LIBERATION AND SELF-ENSLAVEMENT

From the esthetic of spirituality the step to its social ethics is never large. Ancient Hebraic faith, as distinguished from the later Jewish ideology of priestly ritual and sacred land through the omphalos of Zion, has never dissociated life with God from life with neighbor. The question has been, ever since the Hebraic community of the Mosaic covenant, "Who is my neighbor?" The historical roots of this faith through the teaching and life of Jesus, interiorizes the notion of salvation and never forgets its political and economic implications. It is impregnated with the ferment of the great prophets, who already in the eighth century B.C. confronted the kings and their queens, the princesses, the princes, and the priests of Israel with unrelenting severity:

> Hear this word, ye cows of Bashan . . . ,
> Who oppress the poor and crush the needy,
> Who say to your lords,
> Bring wine that we may get drunk! (Amos 4:1).

Even at the court of Jerusalem, the aristocratic Isaiah, perhaps a member of the royal family, complained and predicted,

> The land is filled with silver and gold . . . ,
> But the pride of men shall be brought low (Isa 2:7,11).

The irony of all revolutions shows itself in the moral decay of the revolutionaries themselves. The sons and daughters of the liberated slaves have enslaved others in their turn. However, the ethics of justice which the great prophets inspired could not be confused with human techniques of violence. The poet of the Magnificat took the long view of history. A perspective of time was not abrogated by the eschatological fever which seized the church. Waiting for the day of the Lord, the followers of the living Jesus were enabled to discern the inner working of justice from generation to generation. They knew that their God

> Pours contempt on princes
> And looses the belt of the strong . . . ,
> Takes away understanding from the nations of the earth,
> And makes them stagger like drunk men (Job 12:21,24).

The poet of the Magnificat was the mouthpiece of the early Christian hope. The *Anamnesis*—the recollection of the Name (vs 49*b*)—prepares the reform of the society as if it were already part of the eucharistic ceremonial. The singing of "The Holy One Is His Name" functions as a counterpoint to the Sanctus of holy communion, already sung by the seraphim at the call of Isaiah:

> Holy, holy, holy is Yahweh, the Lord of Hosts (Isa 6:3).

Centuries ahead of the Sanctus in the liturgy of the eucharist, the Magnificat sensed that the holiness of the Name in history led to the theology of God's compassion when such a theology includes a broad, universal, and also internal source of power in humanity. Those who fear him in love are individuals from all races and in all climes who face the decision to live anew for the sake of their community. As Isaiah had already discovered in the eighth century B.C., Jerusalem was no longer a privileged sanctuary for priests officiating on behalf of special people. With the holiness of the Name, Isaiah learned that not Zion but "the entire earth is filled with [God's] glory" (Isa 6:3*b*). The knowledge both of God's "awe-fulness" and of his "world-wide-fullness" brought the prophet to an awareness of corporate guilt and solidarity with the sinfulness of his own nation (vs 5). Salvation led

immediately to apostolate, in the primitive meaning of ambassador-
ship: "Whom shall I send?" (vs 8).

Failure to respond to the demands of holiness produces a vicious
circle of pride, arrogance, possessiveness, and empty phantasmagoria.

The core-verse of the Magnificat elliptically joins the nature of
divine power, disguised through a secret "in-fleshing" within the
womb of a simple woman, to the momentous activity of the God of
justice. Yahweh no longer dispatches his heavenly hosts against the
tyrants of the earth, according to the ancient myth of the "warrior-
god." Rather, he initiates the use of psychological warfare. He plots
their mental disintegration. "He has scattered the proud in the imagination of their hearts" (vs 52b).

III. MENTAL DISINTEGRATION

On the surface, this mode of retribution appears ineffectual. Re-
flection upon its significance, however, discloses that such a punish-
ment corresponds to hell on earth. Commentators who claim that the
Magnificat, with its anthological citations from the Hebrew scriptures,
amounts to little more than a tapestry of pious words, fail to point out
that the core-verse, which articulates the whole poem, "He has scattered the proud in the imagination of their hearts," constitutes an un-
precedented insight into the psychological analysis of illusory desire.
The sentence "he has scattered the proud" is reminiscent of an ancient
canticle (Ps 89:10). The words which have been rendered in the
Greek text, *dianoia kardias autôn*, "in the imagination of their hearts,"
were probably borrowed from a late rendition of Solomon's prayer,

> Keep this for ever in the imagination of the thoughts of the
> heart of thy people (1 Chron 29:18).

However, the Magnificat used the expression "the imagination
of their hearts" in the pejorative sense of "device," "plotting,"
"scheming," or even "conceit," especially since the Hebrew word
for "heart" designates, not the seat of emotional or instinctive life,
but intellectual consciousness and human powers of autonomous
reasoning.

The wealth accumulated by the proud, as depth-psychology has shown in modern times, is the symbol of their fear of annihilation. I amass material goods before I melt into nothingness. My pride and particularly my ignorance are the manifestations of my refusal to accept my mortality. I seek power over my fellow beings whenever eternal assurance fails me. Hell is a dead end and a present void when enjoyment of social status through riches becomes—temporarily—a substitute for ephemerality. I am dying, therefore I desire to extend my finitude. What I acquire, in the long run, is the knowledge of my own destitution. The man and the woman in the myth of the Garden eat the fruit of absolute knowledge in order to be like God and to live forever. They only discover that they are naked! "He has scattered the proud in the imagination of their hearts."

In pre-Elizabethan English, imagination was taken almost always in the sense of vacuous or savage fancy. King Lear begs for an ounce of civet to sweeten his imagination. And Hamlet exclaims, "My imaginations are as foul as Vulcan's stithy." The God who is praised in the Magnificat does not hurl his thunderbolt at the potentates of the earth but satisfies them with the fulfillment of their lust to possess what ultimately amounts to an "airy nothing."

IV. THE REVERSAL OF DESTINY

The third strophe (vss 52–53) inserts into Christian ethics the theological critique of political systems that favor the rich at the expense of the poor. The Magnificat has distilled in two couplets the dramatic plea of the great prophets of Israel for social justice. Amos, Hosea, Isaiah, Micah, and Jeremiah were the forerunners of Jesus, not because they predicted a Messiah but because they condemned corrupt monarchs and their princes, their priests, and their minions.

At Passover, Israel celebrates her liberation from foreign slavery, but this liberation has not led to the unshackling of her self-enslavement. When the church claims to be the true Israel, the church falls into the same kind of blindness and self-deception. Human nature is finite, but infinitely shrewd. In the end, it may be infinitely idiotic. The sons and daughters of liberated slaves are enslaving their own sisters and brothers. Their perspective of time, the glow of their vocation, and the unique sense of solidarity in communality should have enabled them to discern the inner working of justice from generation to generation. Their poets knew that the God of the Sinai covenant would in some way "lift the needy from the ash-heap and make them sit with the princes" (1 Sam 2:8). They hoped for an era of harmonious corporateness. So stated the psalmist who intoned the song of Hannah, Samuel's mother. Her words are now borrowed, centuries later, by the poet of the Magnificat. Yet, the difference between the two poems should not be overlooked. The Magnificat does not say unqualifiedly, "The Lord makes poor and he makes rich" (1 Sam 2:7). The power of Mary's God aims at the eradication of unrighteousness. He is not responsible for new iniquities.

The rhythm of the third strophe is now dictated by a dramatic use of double chiasmus with the verbs "he put down" and "he exalted," "he filled to satiety" and "he sent empty away." Ensconced in the long tradition of "the poor of Israel," the poet gave fresh life to the perspective of hope, and the spectacular contrasts of Hannah's hymn, but he did so in the context of motivated retribution. Hannah had sung:

> [Yahweh] . . . reduces to lowliness and he lifts up,
> He raises the needy from the dust
> And the poor from the dung-heap
> To seat them with potentates
> And make them inherit a throne of glory
> (1 Sam 2:7–8a).

The poet of the Magnificat, however, modified his model through the pungent wisdom of the sages who taught the poet of Job:

> [God] leads princes away spoiled
> And overthrows the mighty (Job 12:19).

He also espouses the vigorous denunciation of the prophets, who had prayed,

Reduce the proud to lowliness
And exalt the man of low degree (Ezek 21:26 [Heb 31]).

In addition to a reversal of social status, the poet remembers the famished who are waiting for the great feast that was already expected by the psalmist,

He fills the soul of the hungry with good things (Ps 107:9*b*).

The end of the stanza returns, nevertheless, to the theme of the core-verse when it makes concrete the psychological void of the heart,

But the rich he sent empty away.

The Magnificat predicts in no uncertain terms the eventual end of any civilization that cultivates material pleasures at the expense of an ethic of sharing. Although they represent only a fraction of the population of the entire planet, the industrial states today devour altogether a third of the total amount of natural resources. They might learn from the Magnificat that the day of reckoning cannot be far distant, but they are lulled by the conceit of their technology, which springs from "the imagination of their hearts." The Magnificat accuses us, not without animus, not without justification.

The third strophe offers a hard saying. Mary appears in its strains no longer as the sweet mother of traditional piety. She is now made to speak in concert with the oppressed wives and the famished mothers of the world.

The esthetics of spirituality in singing call for an ethic of an abrupt social upheaval and reordering.

V. MUSICAL ILLUSTRATIONS

CORE-VERSE

51. *Fecit potentiam in brachio suo:*
     Dispersit superbos mente cordis sui.

Strophe III

52. *Deposuit potentes de sede,*
     Et exaltavit humiles.
53. *Esurientes implevit bonis*
     Et divites dimisit inanes.

Until the nineteenth century musicians, with few exceptions, were relegated to servants' quarters along with domestic helpers and sideline entertainers. Particularly sensitive to economic and social humiliation, they could easily sympathize with the poor, since they were themselves retainers of the church hierarchy or of the potentates of secular principalities. The violent style of the core-verse and of the third strophe must have appealed to the musical interpreters.

1. *Claudio Monteverdi* (1567-1643) was court composer for the Duke of Mantua. He published in 1610 two Magnificats: a Magnificat Primo, for seven voices, with flamboyant orchestration, and a Magnificat for six voices, more subtle and in parts as ethereal as any piece of an earlier age. In this composition, only three voices are used for the *Fecit potentiam* (vs 51) and the *Deposuit* (vss 52-53). Two soprano voices sing in melismatic echo, as if to convey with levity a playfulness of rejoicing at the fall of tyrants, but its *Schadenfreude* is darkened by the sadness of the tenor who maintains the Cantus at a level of inexorable horizontality. The fate of the mighty in this world is already at hand. Justice will be stern, but reasoned and stable. Is the third voice announcing that we are already gone from the earthly scene? Is glamor only a vision in the night? A dream that is past? A moth at the flame?

By contrast, the *Esurientes*, when the famished will be fed at the heavenly banquet with the good things they long for, is couched at first in short notes, with modulations of jollity. But it soon makes room for the *divites* who slowly, in spite of their riches, are sent away empty, *inanes*.

2. *Johann Sebastian Bach* (1685-1750) allowed his sense of drama to color the melodic line and the orchestral accompaniment

for a relentless evocation of the doom that confronts a materialistic civilization. A tenor voice announces the advent of the revolution, but a mezzo soprano enunciates the feeding of the hungry. Might it be that Bach did not hesitate, at least once, to picture Mary not only as a prophet of strict justice but also as the *Mater Genetrix* and the *Alma Mater*, both the Mother who brings forth and the Mother who nurtures?

The *Fecit potentiam* mobilizes the entire chorus and the full orchestra, but the *Dispersit*, ending on a diminished seventh chord at *superbos*, leads to the misty emptiness of *mente cordis sui* and its unexpected adagio. A tenor aria requiring vocal gymnastics is introduced by descending chromatic phrases for the violins. The mood is intense, laborious, almost fierce, as if Bach not only sympathized with the plight of the fallen princes but also sensed the near-embarrassment of the sovereign Judge, who has to execute such drastic retribution against an elite of corrupt nobility. Hesitation yields, however, to decisiveness. God may hesitate, but the deed must be performed. *Deposuit potentes de sede*. In its first phrase, the revolution from on high topples the potentates from their thrones, but the descent of notes leads also later to a joyful ascent. *Exaltavit*, like the young mother's *Exultavit* of the first strophe, raises the humble and the poor from their low estate. This is the second phase of the revolution, when the famished are invited to the festive banquet in the kingdom of God. *Esurientes*, an aria sung by an alto solo, is accompanied by two flutes over a contrasting obbligato of plucked strings in the contrabass, soothing, yet ominously muted.

The last bars remind the rich of their vanity. The flutes play on a parallel line of thirds up to the end of the cadence. Then something quite unanticipated occurs. The final note of the melody is missing. This is the master's way of saying *inanes, inanes*. The tonal resolution is absent. We are left in mid-air, frustrated, our ears begging for the satisfaction of our musical sense. It is not there. We face the void. Bach knew the meaning of heaven, but also of hell—nothing.

3. *Michael Tippett* (b. 1905). This contemporary British composer does not belong to any school. He is neither a classicist nor a serialist. His *Magnificat* was composed for the choir of St. John's at Cambridge. The text is sung in English (King James Version). An

opening blast of organ pipes with shattering dissonances stresses a swift ascension of notes on the tromba stop. Brutally, but effectively, Tippett modernizes the traditional Anglican chant, at once setting together the swiftness of divine justice and the exaltation of the promise made to Mary.

With short and repeated punctuations from the organ between sung phrases, a full chorus dominates the first strophe and the beginning of the second. Peace and intimacy suddenly come when a soprano voice sings a cappella the confidence in a God who will not abandon humankind, "And his mercy is on them that fear him" (vs 50). Almost at once, however, the chorus returns with torrential thrusts of sound for the core-verse, "He hath shewed strength with his arm" (vs 51). The revolution of God is evoked without compromise, but it becomes a background of rigor for the introduction of the next motif. The theme of the feeding of the hungry slows the pace, softening and illumining the final picture of history, which too soon ends the canticle.

4. *Alan Hovhaness* (b. 1911). Even for the *Fecit potentiam* this contemporary artist preserves the Byzantine style inherited from a pre-Christian Greek mode and from a synagogal chant, as well as ornamented with reminiscences of the Armenian liturgy. Rather than following Baroque interpretation, which depicted the enormity of the social reversal with a vigorous galloping of notes unleashed by the full orchestra, Hovhaness invites an alto solo, surrounded by a heart-rendering melody for trombone and strings. Together, the voice and the brass legato spell out the dirge-like epic of retribution for economic and political abuse of the masses. Centuries of massacres and oppression of the Armenians surge to the threshold of this composer's consciousness. Like Mary, the daughter of Zion, the musician feels the burden of ancestral tortures.

The core-verse flows without pause into the *Dispersit* and the *Deposuit*, but the *Esurientes*, sung by a male chorus, is kept distinct. In free rhythm with strings, it belongs to another, altogether different movement. The musical exegete deliberately breaks apart the two phrases of the revolution in order to emphasize the utter newness of well-being in the ultimate status of humanity. The old world has come to its deserved end. One cannot help lamenting for "the Mighty fallen," but the novelty in the realm of God is like new wine. It deserves a new earth and a new heaven, the wine of guiltless effervescence, without the menace of famine and mortality.

5. *Krzysztof Penderecki* (b. 1933) of Kracow and New Haven, conducted his *Magnificat* when it was first heard in the United States at Carnegie Hall in 1978. Half-tones follow micro-tones in tightly controlled legato, never to be confused with the slurring effect of a glissando. The voice of the basso profundo, however, intones the *Fecit potentiam* in the classical manner, on a single note, repeated several times, rising in pitch and gradually swelling into a fortissimo. It threatens, insists, overturns, crashes, and finally subsides in a low register, to cajole and entice. The composer has understood the crux of the poem in its core-verse, when divine power is transferred from the catastrophes of history to the humble and unknown birth of the new being.

Chapter 5

The Sacrality of the Future

STROPHE IV
(KING JAMES VERSION)

54.   He hath holpen his servant Israel,
        In remembrance of his mercy;
55.   As he spake to our fathers,
        To Abraham, and to his seed
            for ever.

It would be wrong to conclude from an examination of the third strophe that the Magnificat, a biblical theology in miniature, leads to an ideology of revolutionary violence. It calls for a radical reorganization of society, but it does not advocate an eighteenth-century utopianism leading simplistically to the motto, "Liberty, Equality, Fraternity." It accepts the validity of such an ideal and it wants to eradicate the glaring inequalities that characterize the excesses of plutocratic capitalism and imperialism. At the same time, it does not seek justice through the common denominator of forced populism. A symbol of Hebrew-Christian faith in its dynamics, the Magnificat seeks to promote an ethic of communality. It asks for the reversal of privilege by birth and it calls for the reappraisal of nobility, the responsibility of an elite, and the significance of an open church, the true Israel, whose mission is to be "a light unto the nations."

Peoplehood, not the rule of a class privileged from birth, inheritance, or the amassing of riches, is the goal of Hebrew-Christian ethics. Peoplehood, not of race or breed and not separated from the world through the myth of an ancestral election, looks for a true community—the united family of humankind. This goal implies the renewal of an elite in every generation, not an oligarchy or outward power which eventually becomes corrupt, but an aristocracy in the full and primary sense of the word—government by the innermost best, the considerate, the sensitive, the dedicated, the constantly renewable ferment of a steadfastly self-critical organism of worldwide administration.

The Magnificat does not support the view that self-interest and the friction of competitive factions among human beings is the best, however imperfect, modus vivendi for the pluralistic world.

I. A NEW ELITE

The fourth strophe (vss 54–55) winds up the plea for social justice with the reaffirmation of Israel, the chosen people:

He has upheld Israel, his slave-boy (vs 54a).

A poet of the primitive church in Jerusalem lent words to the lips of Mary. He did not for a moment suspect that Israel's mission of responsibility to the world was abrogated. Yet the juxtaposition of the name of the chosen people with the word "slave-boy" inevitably called to the singer's mind the death of the Lord Jesus and by this very fact implied a radical distinction between elitism and elite.

While elitism designates the fossilization of social inequality, and populism seeks the leveling off of all to the lowest drabness of energy and achievement, the Magnificat, true to the theology of the whole Bible, declares that society moves ahead only when it is spearheaded by an authentic aristocracy of the spirit. It endorses the seminal function of a few for the attainment of greatness as it filters to the many.

Greatness is a strange quality. It is not an easily reducible reality. There are multifarious diversities of talents and opportunities. "Some are born great, some achieve greatness, and some have greatness thrust upon them."[1]

---

[1] Shakespeare, *Twelfth Night*, ii, 5, 149–51.

Madonna of the Chair

The slave-boy Israel has greatness thrust upon him, just as Mary has greatness thrust upon her. Some Italian Renaissance painters of the annunciation have often represented her as shrinking from the angel's summons. She foresees the burden within the honor, the sorrow under the joy, the horrors of the end. The annunciation prefigures the *Pietà*. Mary "full of grace" is already the *Mater Dolorosa*.

A modern poet might have lent these words to Mary addressing her yet-unborn child:

> I carry you inside me
> like the memory of my ancestors.
> For years, for eons,
> I have known how you feel,
> exactly the tiny weight
> of you against my breast,
> the small indentation
> beneath your wispy hair,
> warm, filled with scents
> of sunshine and new grass.
> Swollen with love and pain
> I know you better
> than I know anyone else.
> You wear my sorrow
> around your small head.
> I have whispered your name,
> wept it and crooned it.
> At night
> in the pitch dark
> I have gazed into
> your still, sleeping face,
> the face of my child,
> my dreaming child, my love
> O when will you come?[2]

---

[2] Cécile Terrien Lampton, 1978.

The woman-slave of the Lord accepts, both joyfully and reluctantly, the crown of thorns. So also Israel, the slave-boy of Yahweh throughout the ten centuries of biblical history, and Jesus, the final symbol of the people of God.

Modeling his response on Jeremiah's resistance to the prophetic call (Jer 1:5–6), many a poet, like Paul Verlaine, cried, "I have the ecstasy and the terror of being chosen." The Magnificat, in fact, quotes a disciple of Job and Jeremiah when he states:

[Yahweh] has upheld his slave-boy Israel (vs 54).

To his fellow exiles of 545 B.C., whose parents had been brutally uprooted, religiously benumbed, nationally shamed, and physically starved, the anonymous prophet, composer of the poetry now preserved in the second part of the book of Isaiah (chs. 40–55), sounded the clarion call of the sovereign of the nations:

Behold my slave-boy, whom I uphold (Isa 42:1).

The Greek verb in the Lukan text of the Magnificat (Lk 1:54*a*) borrows the Septuagint rendering of the Hebrew original verb *tamak*, which means "to support and maintain under duress and at great cost." It connotes the idea of "grasping, embracing, seizing firmly" (Exod 17:12; Ps 41:12 [Heb 12]; 63; 8 [Heb 9]; cf. Isa 41:10).

In the Deutero-Isaianic ballads of the servant of Yahweh, the upholding of Israel is inseparable from the theme of election, selection, and therefore predilection.

> Mine elect! In whom my whole being delights!
>   I have put my spirit upon him;
> He shall bring forth true justice to the nations . . .
>   (Isa 42:1).

But the task entrusted to this slave-boy, Israel, was not to instill in those nations a legal structure of justice. The Chosen One of the Lord will respect the diversity of the human conditions. He will deal gently with underprivileged minorities and with the weakest principalities:

A bruised reed will he not crush,
A dimly-lit wick will he not stamp out (Isa 42:3).

II. PREDILECTION

Israel is the chosen people and the people of God's predilection because its *raison d'être* in history is to bring true justice to humanity. The task of Israel is "to be a light unto the nations: namely, to enlighten the world, not only technically and culturally, but also morally and spiritually. This is not to be construed as merely an intellectual illuminating through the spread of philosophical knowledge. It is the awesome task of extending authentic freedom to all,

> To open the eyes of the blind,
> To free captives from prison
> And those who sit in darkness out of their dungeons
> (Isa 42:7).

An elite is a group elected for assuring genuine and therefore inclusive peace. *Shalom*, "peace," is not, in effect, distinct from *shalem*, "health in growth and without exclusiveness." The Indo-European notions of peace—whether the Greek *eirênê*, the Latin *pax*, or the Teutonic *Frieden*—derive from the radical image of "imposing order upon." The Semitic root of *shalom* and its use by the prophets of Israel point to an antithetical notion of coherence from within, not *Pax Babylonica* nor *Pax Romana*, but "the peace that passeth understanding."

The Ballads of the Slave-Boy of the Lord in the Second Isaiah inspired the poet of the Magnificat in such a compelling way that the identity of the slave-boy of the Lord could no longer remain in doubt. The early Christians who sang these songs saw in him the individual who represents Israel in the flesh. The flexibility of this identity was already intended by the Isaianic prophet of the exile, since his climactic song (Isa 52:13–53:12) differentiated between the suffering slave, brought to silent death for the sake of the nations, and "[his] people" (Isa 53:8*d*).

It was without any forcing of the Hebrew scripture that the early Christians recognized in Jesus the slave-boy of the Lord, who was

> Anointed to preach good tidings to the poor . . .
> To proclaim release to the captives . . .
> And recovering sight to the blind,
> To set at liberty those that are bruised,
> To proclaim the acceptable year of the Lord
>   (Lk 4:18–19; cf. Isa 42:7; cf. 61:1–2).

It was a similar interpretation of the song of the Servant that enabled the primitive Jerusalem community to overcome their despair over the death of their master. How could a just man be condemned and executed with common criminals? The answer was provided by scripture: he gave his life "as a ransom for many" (Mk 10:45; cf. Isa 53:10–11).

The first phrase of the fourth strophe of the Magnificat, "He upheld Israel his slave-boy," inevitably brought to mind the embryonic Christology of the nascent church. Jesus had become the incarnation of the true Israel. The notion of true greatness had passed from a collectivity to an individual. Jesus, the fruit of Mary's womb, is the slave-boy whom God chose, grasped, and sustained for the fulfillment of his hidden purpose in history.

The slave-woman of the Lord has conceived the slave-boy of the Lord. True greatness lies in passionate dedication. The mother of the revolution is adumbrated as the *Mater Dolorosa*, the *Pietà* at the foot of the cross. By poetic inclusion from the first to the last strophe, the Magnificat operated a theological transference from Israel to Jesus. It also brought together passion, greatness, and peace.

Marianne Moore put it crisply:

> Pacific yet passionate
> for if not both, how
> could he be great?[3]

---

[3] Marianne Moore, "Leonardo da Vinci" in *The Complete Poems of Marianne Moore* (New York: Macmillan/Viking, 1967), p. 201.

Even a slightly cynical realist like the Duke of La Rochefoucauld could rise to the heights of perceptiveness when he remarked, "Great souls are not those who have less passion and more virtue than the souls of commoners, but those only who entertain great designs, great goals, great purposes."

If the church is heir to Israel, let it be a light unto the nations, and for this aim, let it rediscover, in every generation of humankind, the secret of greatness, which was well expressed by Seneca, a Stoic philosopher,

> *habere fragilitatem hominis, securitatem dei* (to have the fragility of a man and the security of a god).

The mystery of the holy infant, "born of woman" (Gal 4:4), who yet "will be called the Son of the Most High" (Lk 1:32a) does not lie in what later theologians defined as the paradox of his two natures. The Semitic idiom, "son of . . . ," "daughter of . . . ," does not refer to physiological procreation. It carries with it the connotation of similarity, or mirror-reflection, and at best of sequential causation. To call Jesus "the Son of the Most High" is to develop the initial proclamation, "He will be great" (Lk 1:32a).

The singers of the Magnificat were satisfied with the poetic resonances of the phrase, "Israel my slave-boy." They had no need to argue about the mode by which Jesus originated from God. They did not speculate on his supernatural conception, nor on his two wills, nor on his two natures, as later theologians steeped in Hellenistic philosophy did with fanatic zeal. The poetry of the Magnificat would not tear Christendom apart through civil wars on account of heretics accused of Arianism in the Byzantine age and of Socianism in the seventeenth century.

Since the earliest church was a mere grouplet within the vast congregation of Jewry, it was potentially explosive to identify Jesus—a single man denounced and executed as a seditionist—with "Israel, my slave-boy." Such an ascription in effect deprived the Jewish people as a whole of their privileged status of divine predilection. It drove a wedge within the Jewish collectivity. By conferring upon Jesus the

Isaianic motif of "the Servant of the Lord," the singing of the Magnificat affirmed his security over his frailty. It also extended to his followers the quality of true Israel, whose members were embraced in the new beingness. In spite of their poverty and of their being ostracized, they stood upon the certitude of an eternal destiny.

The duality of their conviction of frailty and security was the source of their triumphant character. Weak, they conquered misfortune and even the fear of death. Witness of this inward strength, for example, could be seen in the late medieval motto, *Firmus in Terra, Ad Coelum Securus*, "Firm on earth, secure toward heaven" (1476).

To be sure, the poet of the Magnificat did not consciously intend such a breadth of interpretation, but the Lukan context of the gospel of the infancy made imperiously convincing the suggestiveness of the phrase, "He upheld Israel, his slave-boy." The early Christians were devout Jews who read their scriptures as a disclosure, support, and confirmation of their new *raison d'être*.

III. ANTICIPATION

The transfer of the human faculty of memory to the divine person is one of the primary characteristics of Hebrew faith. According to the poet of the Magnificat, the fidelity of God from generation to generation of tortuous history upheld Israel, his slave-boy, because he remembered his motherly compassion.

The notion of compassionate memory was traditional in Hebraism and much later also in Jewry. In this respect, as well as in others, the Magnificat is tributary to this tradition. Yet, once again, it must be observed that the inspiration from ancient scriptures produced not a passive imitation but an innovative freedom and in fact an original recreation.

The psalmists had hailed the God who

> . . . remembered his mercy to Jacob,
> And his trust for the house of Israel
> (Ps 98:3[LXX]),

and the musician who composed at the dawn of the Roman age
affirmed that,

> The Lord will remember his servants in mercy
> (Ps Sol 10:4*a*).

However, the poet of the Magnificat did not select the word
chesed, "mercy," or "covenant lovingkindness," but chose the bold
and stunning notion of *rachmim*, "motherly longings," which he had
already used in the second strophe (vs 50). Just as he paired the slave-
boy of the final stanza with the slave-woman of the first (vs 48), so
also he insisted on intertwining the two motifs by repeating the word
rachmim, "compassion of the womb," in order to emphasize the sustained will of God to save his children.

The attribution of "memory" to the Deity continues the anthro-
pomorphic language which has been noted throughout the Magnificat. The ancient Hebrews often spoke of forgetting and remembering
in connection with both man and God. A later Jewish saying affirmed,
"He who does not remember that God led *him* out of Egypt is no
longer a Jew."

It is the Hebraic insight of remembering the exodus as a present
experience reenacted each year in the ritual of Passover which informs
most forcefully the eucharistic ritual.

From a human recollection of grace, the sense leaps to divine
remembrance. The *anamnesis* of the Lord's supper is the refusal to let
the past be forgotten. It is also the determination to anticipate the
future and to enact the last day as if it had already arrived. Memory is
at once commemoration and anticipation.

In the conception of the Holy Child, the long history of God's
yearning for all his children on earth comes to its supreme moment.
On account of his word in time past, God now acts out his word for all
times to come. "Soon we ourselves shall stand on the horizon of the
following generation. Meanwhile the horizon recedes, and the world
that seemed ended begins anew."[4]

---

[4] Marcel Proust, *Time Regained*, III, p. 929.

The secular prose of Marcel Proust is an indirect testimony to the vitality of Hebrew-Christian dynamics. Remembrance is constantly adjusted in order to remain a prediction. It anticipates a changed humanity. Apotheosis is the display of God's passion to effectuate human metamorphosis. "Drinking from a cup of shadows," God, with womb-like longings, whispers reconciliation among races, creeds, nations, and men and women everywhere.

IV. THE PROGENY OF ABRAHAM

In the remembrance of his compassion, God solemnly declares the sacrality of the future and the universality of his promise.

> As he spoke to our fathers,
> To Abraham, and to his seed for ever (vs 55).

Divine speech is articulation of God's presence. It proclaims his will to save those who belong to the spiritual descendance of Abraham.

The Magnificat is a biblical theology in miniature, because it begins and it ends in an exaltation not of Mary but of the Word. It has been said, especially in recent years, that scriptural religion leads to babbling rather than to contemplation. This charge reflects a distorted view of both Jewry and Christendom. It does not address the cardinal character of the Hebrew-Christian dynamics of faith. Historians of comparative religions have observed that the many cults of the world favor either the eye or the ear. Those that stress the visual element tend to foment a static conservatism, a stagnant immobilism, in social ethics as well as in individual spirituality. Those that insist upon the auditive faculty almost always generate forces of change, provide a broad perspective of history, and incite growth within individuals and communities.

The former produce a religion of the *icon*, which always carries the risk of a mystical identification with nature. The latter ignites the passion for seeking the improvement of human society.

Like the literature of the great prophets and the proverbs and parables of the sages, the early traditions concerning Abraham and Moses promoted a theology of the Word, for the God who "spoke"

with them could not be "seen." The priests of Jerusalem, partly influenced by the old Canaanite cult and allied to the Davidic dynasty,
supported a theology of a "glory" which could be seen in the temple
of Zion.

Martin Buber correctly remarked, "The Jew of antiquity—i.e.,
the pre-exilic Hebrew—was more acoustically oriented than visually,
and more temporally oriented than spatially."[5]

The descendants of the Jerusalem priests eventually presided
over the birth of Judaism during and after the exile in Babylon. The
whole expression and practice of fidelity to Yahweh was centered in
the temple of Zion, where the glory of the Lord was believed to reside.

The poet of the Magnificat was a theologian of the Word. When
he referred to God's speaking to the fathers (vs 55), he proposed a
subtle correspondence with his previous declaration on the holiness of
the Name (vs 49). The Word became the key-motif of Christian faith.
The prologue of the fourth gospel integrates the theology of the Word
with the awesome uniqueness of the man Jesus: "And the Word was
made flesh" (Jn 1:14). For the early Christians, the sanctuary was
empty and desolate (Lk 13:35), whereas Jesus went to his death in
glory (Jn 1:14). The temple became a metaphor of the living church,
the ongoing community of the living Lord.

Not only does the fourth strophe of the Magnificat celebrate the
sacrality of the future, but it also proclaims the universality of Abraham's descendance, no longer of race but of allegiance.

> In thee, all the families of the earth shall seek their mutual
> welfare (Gen 12:3).

John the Baptist rightly interpreted the Abrahamic ideology when
he cut open the genetic exclusivism of his time, saying that even the
stones in his path could be raised by God as sons and daughters of
Abraham (Lk 3:8). In an almost imperceptible way, the final lines of
the Magnificat are still expecting the revolution, but they do so within
the perspective of time, and they select not violence but persuasion

---

from inside the human psyche. This is the reason for which the song of Mary ends with the evocation of Abraham, the father of the faith. The seminal elite is not restricted to those who claim a nobility of birth or the correctness of ritual. It gathers from the whole of humankind those who accept an affinity with the Christ, inheritor of the prophets of Israel,

> . . . weaving the sublime
> proportions
> Of a true monarch's
> soul . . . .

To them the same mysterious God repeats, age after age,

> Ye shall be
> The salt of all the elements, world of the world.[6]

Equality of opportunity among all men and women does not mean egalitarianism, for a new elite arises from the rank and file of every generation.

The miracle of Jonah, as Jesus read it, was that the Ninevites repented (Lk 11:30-32). The followers of the living Lord spread like wildfire among the ethnic and economic victims of Roman military imperialism, because in Christ "there is neither Jew nor Greek" (Gal 3:28). The belief in an Abraham genetic filiation through Ishmael—for the Arabs—or through Isaac—for the Jews—should not in any way preclude the validity of a Christian grafting into the Abraham tree (Rom 11:17-24).

> Those who are great are those who cease to believe in neatly connected events.[7]

---

[6] Ralph W. Emerson, *Poems, Complete Works* (Boston and New York: Houghton Mifflin, 1911), IX pp. 381-2.

[7] Quoted in Everett Hoffmann, "Mommssen's Rome," *New York Times,* June 26, 1972, p. 32.

This opinion of an eminent pagan, Lucius Cornelius Sulla, applies to the spiritual progeny of Abraham.

The true sons and daughters of the man from Ur, be they Jewish, Christian, or Muslim, are "the uneasy ones with crust broken." The elect have renounced their immunities. They live with "a heart exercised in responsibility," wrote Amos Wilder.[8] "The veiled symbols of vocation and promise will be their native tongue." The Abraham elite is to be judged by the standard of excellence, for upon them rests the survival of humankind. The Magnificat affirms the future.

V. MUSICAL ILLUSTRATIONS

Strophe IV

54. *Suscepit Israel puerum suum,*
     Recordatus misericordiae suae,
55. *Sicut locutus est ad patres nostros,*
     Abraham, et semini ejus in saecula.

The fourth strophe of the Magnificat reviews in a concise sweep the whole history of salvation from Abraham to the end of time. Musicians of the Magnificat have often used for this climactic ending meditative and sustained lines, which unobtrusively shift into fugues, and little by little accelerate into a tempo of hope. They seek with near impatience, as it were, to hasten the triumph of God "for ever."

1. *Andrea Gabrieli* (1510–1586) in Renaissance Venice was praised by his nephew, Giovanni Gabrieli (1557–1612), for expressing the brilliance of the liturgy with a reticence of emotion. In the *Suscepit Israel puerum suum,* we are submerged within a sea of sound, through which the epic of the chosen people unfolds from military conquest to military defeat and yet to inward triumph. The words of the anonymous prophet of the exile in Babylon, when all seems to be lost, sing like the act of faith and its "nevertheless."

---

[8] Amos Wilder, *Theology and Literature* (Cambridge: Harvard, 1968), p.10.

The three choirs provide an amplitude of voices, supported by organ and brass, which convincingly present the paradox of the *Deus Absconditus*, self-concealed but still in control, whose emissary on earth is a suffering slave. This figure is not just Israel as a people deprived of land but as a society strengthened in spirit. It also designates a mysterious individual, whose name has been lost from the memory of nascent Judaism, after Cyrus the Mede permitted the early Jews to return.

The anonymity of the silent servant allowed the early Christians to "type" the uniqueness of the man, Jesus of Nazareth. In the final phrases of this motif, Gabrieli indicates his perception of Israel's sublimity: the suffering and the death of the Lamb of God, *Agnus Dei* (Isa 53:7).

2. *Johann Sebastian Bach* (1685–1750). As in Advent and at Christmas, the mystery of rebirth announces the mystery of the cross and of the rebirth. Johann Sebastian Bach elected to assign the phrase *He hath upholden his servant Israel* to a trio of feminine voices, no doubt suggestive of the three women who, according to the Johannine gospel (Jn 19:25), stood at the foot of the cross—Mary, the wife of Cleophas, Mary Magdalene, and Mary, the *Mater Dolorosa*.

Some historians think that at the beginning of the eighteenth century the medieval custom of rocking a doll, symbol of the Holy Infant, persisted in Lutheran Saxony.[9] Worshippers carried this doll in their arms, while softly singing a lullaby that was also almost a lament. Bach's *Suscepit Israel puerum suum* combines the epic with the elegiac style. He understood that the celebration of the nativity anticipated the passion.

Preparing the last line of the *Magnificat* on the progeny of Abraham (vs 55), Bach adapted the *Tonus Peregrinus* traditionally used by pilgrims on the night of Tenebrae (before or after Good Friday), while they completed the stations of the cross barefooted and on their knees. The *Tonus Peregrinus* appears in a choral form through the long notes of two oboes.

---

[9] Albert Schweitzer, *J. S. Bach*, tr. Ernest Newman (London: Adam & Charles Black, 1911), II, p. 167 and note.

In his first setting of the *Magnificat*, sung at the Thomaskirche in Leipzig on Christmas Day, 1723, Bach employed the ninth tone, the *Tonus Peregrinus*, which was that of Psalm 113, *In exitu Israel* (Ps 114 in the Hebrew and modern versions). He performed here one of his feats of exegetical symbolism and he did this on three levels. First, he understood that the *Suscepit* was a quotation from the Isaianic prophet of the exile in Babylon (Isa 42:1); second, the reference to the slave-boy as Israel was viewed as renewing the motif of the exodus from Egypt; and third, the silent servant of the Lord, anonymous instrument of Israel's redemption (Isa 53:4–6), now evokes the darkness of Calvary.

The Jews who became the earliest Christians understood the death of Jesus as a ritual assimilation with self-death and a rebirth into eternal life. So also the *Tonus Peregrinus* of the Passover psalm, commemorating the night of the exodus, was associated with the *Tonus Peregrinus* of Tenebrae. It became the prelude to the Easter theology of the inner-life exodus. Bach suggests that the *Magnificat* offered a programmatic mold for the liberation of men and women from their existential finitude, with its implications of a propensity to evil and mortality. As in the original *Magnificat in E Flat* of 1723, the *Grand Magnificat in D Major* maintains the somber overtones of liberation from the present inner slavery toward triumph over death.

The three women standing at the foot of the cross represent all bereaved mothers, lonely widows, and abandoned wives. The trio of voices sings for the pierced, heart-torn sisters of the Pietà. The emergence of Luther's chorale within the chorus that follows is Bach's method of proclaiming that Jesus, the incarnation of Israel in history, is put to death but is still marching on, ahead of Abraham's progeny. The eternal nomad is the existential man, transformed into the redeeming nomad, the *Peregrinus* of the human quest for an eternal home.

In the *Sicut locutus*, which issues inevitably from the *Recordatus* and explains the *misericordiae*, the memory of divine compassion prepares the paradigm of human loyalty whenever it is confronted by recurrent tragedy. The staggered voices, supported by the contrabass, bring to reality the countless generations "B.C." and "A.D." The fugal form expresses divine purpose. History goes somewhere. The bass

notes evoke the solidity of the ground for the belief in God's engagement. These notes soon open up. They rise to heights of sound as if
they were becoming the *Hosannah in Excelsis* which crowns the *Sanctus* in the vision of the prophet Isaiah (6:1–8), as it does in the *B Minor
Mass*, where the liturgy of the Lord's supper marks the entrance of the
divine into the hearts of the communicants.

The five voices may symbolize Abraham and his progeny facing
the triad of the Trinity. The enlargement of harmonies prefigures the
final *Gloria*. The fugal tempo proceeds straight forward, for history
goes toward its end.

Some nineteenth-century musicologists like Carl Friedrich
Zelter have found in the *Sicut locutus* contrapuntal irregularities.[10]
But they have failed to perceive that Bach-the-theologian was at times
compelling Bach-the-musician to accept and to endure a composi-
tional weakness in order to convey a theological idea. In this case, he
perhaps wanted to show that the *opus Dei* does not unfold without the
horrors of war and catastrophe. Progress is marred with numberless
occurrences of regression, impairing the march of humanity toward a
better world.

No embroidery distracts from the single line of *Abraham et
semini ejus*. The single thread unravels and swiftly falls: *in saecula*.

3. *Giovanni-Battista Sammartini* (1701–1775). Son of a
French oboist who emigrated to Italy, Giovanni Sammartini became
at an early age *maestro di cappella* in the Jesuit church of San Fidele
in Milan. At the height of his career he was serving more than eight
Milan churches in various capacities. His *Magnificat*, probably written
in 1771, stands out among many other similar compositions of the late
Baroque age, for it is treated with a great sobriety of effects, a solemnity
of mood, and a rectilinearity of liturgical phrasing.

A rare unity of musical conception brings together the various
movements, which alternate between a limited chorus of four voices
and a solo aria for soprano or alto. One feels constantly the presence
of the expectant mother with her highest hopes and her premonitions

---

[10] "He would have liked . . . the fifth voice more correctly introduced." *Ibid.*, p. 168.

of sorrow. Almost continuously, but interrupted by moments of absolute silence, a solo trumpet sustains a single note that dominates a soft
accompaniment. The musical exegete knows that the *opus Dei* is not
accomplished without a background of worldly activities.

The rhythm and tempo remain lively for most of the *Magnificat*,
but the pace slackens for the *Suscepit Israel*, as a quartet conveys a
sense of quiet security. The musician exteriorizes the trust exhibited by
the poet in the fourth strophe. The steadiness of God's mercy persists
throughout history. Yet, the tempo accelerates with the *Sicut locutus*,
and the name *Abraham, Abraham*, repeated between two moments
of awesome silence, produces an effect of suspense that may conceal
tentativeness, and perhaps the threat of doubt, just before the final
amplitude of the last words, *et semini ejus in saecula.*

After a brief instrumental introduction, the *Gloria* is given not to
a chorus but to a contralto solo—sung in this recording by the aptly
named Wanda Madonna, of La Scala in Milan. The praise of the
Father, the Son and the Holy Spirit sums up the whole theme of the
Magnificat. Like Piero della Francesca's *Madonna del Parto*, in the
cemetery chapel of Monterchi in the Apennines, who stands great with
child at the entrance of the tabernacle, Sammartini's *Gloria* evokes the
triumph of life over death, when the divine invades humanity. The
Milanese composer captured the meaning of the incarnation—*Deus
in Carne.*

4. *Carl Philipp Emanuel Bach* (1717–1788). In the *Magnificat*
which he wrote at Potsdam in 1749, Carl Philipp Emanuel Bach remains loyal to his father's genius. Yet his *Suscepit Israel* cannot conceal the atmosphere of a new era, which began toward the middle of
the eighteenth century, with its so-called *style galant* and new sensi-
bility (*Empfindsamkeit*). The Baroque was turning into the Rococo in
all its manifestations of art—in architecture, with the ornate churches
of Bavaria, as in the *fantaisie* landscapes of Watteau and the *fantaisie*
portraits of Fragonard. A gradual skepticism about the benevolence of
nature and the enlightenment of reason was penetrating music at the
same time. Fear and attraction of darkness began to pervade the for-
malizations of beauty.

To be sure, the pathos of the Magnificat in Vivaldi and Sammartini, as well as in Johann Sebastian Bach, was inspired by the historical realism of the Bible. Yet, even more than the *Suscepit Israel* of his father, the *Suscepit Israel* of Carl Philipp Emanuel betrays an emotion of profound sadness. Nevertheless, this emotion was restrained in such a way that sadness made room for gravity and for a solemnity of expectation. Hope was hovering over the temptation to despair. The alto aria of the *Suscepit* achieved for the church a holy marriage between the playfulness of an Italian Baroque minuet and the pre-Romantic boldness of a 3/4 march, with its irresistible movement toward resolution. Once again, it may be asserted that the exegesis of the musician arose from an intimate perusal of the biblical text. It linked the slave-boy and the slave-woman with God's compassion that was spoken to the Fathers for the sake of Abraham's progeny. The various themes of the final strophe are brought together in musical coherence and tightness of phrasing.

The *Suscepit* leads immediately to the *Sicut locutus est*, which then expands broadly into the *Abraham et semini ejus in saecula*.

Postscript—The New Creation

The Magnificat is not a haphazard composition. It is a model of what genuine poetry should be. In the words of John Donne, "it contracts the immensities."

The core-verse and its four strophes—two which precede and two which follow—contain the whole sweep of biblical faith, concentrated into an artistic medium of sobriety, and combining lyrical emotion with epic drama. It evokes the entire confession of Hebrew-Christian faith, from Abraham to Jesus Christ and on till the end of the world.

A Hebrew psalm of praise par excellence, the song of Mary claims that victory is assured for the historical experiment which the God of the ages is staging on the planet Earth. But victory always implies a fight. The combat adumbrated by this poem is not a cosmic engagement between the forces of harmony in nature and the threat of chaos, as in the myths of oriental and classical antiquity. The fight lies rather in that man is infinitely prone to evil. By her sturdy faith, Mary, the singer, reveals that life brooks no determinism. The Christian story is "the true and lively myth" (*muthos*) which tells the renewal of the human character.

The misery of man and woman will cease. Destiny is not frozen. Suffering will not be sought or cultivated as a cure. Nevertheless, the mystery of the man Jesus, born of a woman, "Son of the Most High," places death and rebirth at the center of the human drama. Grief will be transmuted into serenity, as coal into diamond and iron ore into pure gold. This is why the Christ calls for the turnabout of human conduct and the birth of the New Being.

The Mary of the Magnificat announces the revolution, but revolution begins in the human heart. Grace from God is the beginning of the new beingness for the one and the many. When we hear the silver trumpets at the end of Johann Sebastian Bach's *Grand Magnificat in D*, we remember the lines of Gerard Manley Hopkins,

In a flash, at a trumpet crash,
I am all at once what Christ is, since he was what I am, and
This Jack, this joke, poor potsherd, patch, matchwood,
    immortal diamond,
        Is immortal diamond.[1]

The song of Mary gives articulation to the necessary link between social justice and individual dedication. It also confers upon life on earth a dimension of impassioned service and of happiness for the human race.

MUSICAL ILLUSTRATION

Musicians of the Magnificat have understood the text. Some of them have fully captured its opalescent resonances and responded to its vision of God, the supreme judge—"supreme" in all his humble sublimity.

The *Gloria*, which concludes most liturgical settings of the Magnificat, does not belong to the text of the Lukan poem. Yet, its traditional use in the course of the centuries has made it an integral part of Vespers (Evensong). Johann Sebastian Bach, a devout Lutheran, showed his catholicity of taste as well as the breadth of his theological faith when he composed for his *Magnificat in D Major* a trinitarian finale, which confers upon the whole work a masterful touch befitting its already monumental symmetry.

---

[1] "That Nature is a Heraclitean Fire and of the Comfort of the Resurrection," *Poems of Gerard Manley Hopkins*, Robert Bridges, ed. (London: Oxford, 1918, 1941), p. 67.

Like some of his predecessors, Bach divided the poem into twelve movements and constructed his musical composition as an architectural succession of twelve architraves that answer one another in couplets. The first movement is echoed by the twelfth: the second by the eleventh; the third by the tenth, etc.; and the core is constituted by the twinned sixth and seventh. Each of these paired couplets is written in the same key. A whole theological interpretation of the poem in its tonality arises from the parallelism of motifs, at first discernible only through the musical structure. Thus, the *Et exultavit* finds its expansion in the *Sicut locutus*, and one discovers that the spirit of the singer (second movement) becomes attuned to the spirit of the savior, who has spoken to our fathers (penultimate movement). A most telling and indeed compelling argument for the view that Bach saw a correspondence between the woman-slave and the boy-slave arises from the identity of key between the *Ancillae suae* of the *Quia respexit* (vs 48) and the *Puerum suum* of the *Suscepit* (vs 54).

Thus the *Gloria*, or twelfth movement, revives the orchestral sweep of the opening Symphonia, the introduction to the chorus in which each voice in turn jubilantly shouts the word *"magnificat."* The phrases mount from the bass to the tenor to the alto to the soprano, in slowly ascending triplets—possibly the source of the last movement of Brahms' *Requiem*—and the three categories of time, with its past, present, and future, are encompassed in a tempo of steady acceleration.

Within the *Gloria*, the *Sicut erat in principio* obviously has to return to the beginning of the *Magnificat*, but this last motif is not a simple repetition of the first. As a profound theologian and an assiduous reader of scripture,[2] Bach did not subscribe to a cyclical view of time, illustrated so eloquently, so nostalgically, and in the end so despairingly by Mircea Eliade in *The Eternal Return*.[3] The view of a

---

[2] William H. Scheide, *Johann Sebastian Bach as Biblical Interpreter* (Princeton: Princeton Theological Seminary, 1952); Jacques Chailley, *Les Passions de J. S. Bach* (Paris: Presses Universitaires, 1963); Jaroslav Pelikan, *Bach Among the Theologians* (Philadelphia: Fortress, 1986). That Bach did not passively accept the poetic texts and biblical selections made by others is evident from the marginal notes he wrote in his copy of scriptures. See Howard H. Cox, ed., *The Calov Bible of J. S. Bach* (Ann Arbor, MI: UMI Research Press, 1985).

[3] M. Eliade, *Cosmos and History: The Myth of the Eternal Return* (New York: Harper & Bros., 1954), pp. 86–90; 126–130, with Eliade's misunderstanding of genuine Chistianity.

history that repeats itself forever belongs to religions of the east and of classical antiquity, but Hebrew-Christian scriptures alone, which "recorded" the persistence of the divine mercy—*"Recordatus misericordiae suae, Sicut locutus est ad patres nostros"*—dispels the despondency that floats on stagnant ponds. Montaigne's *"branloire perenne"* (perennial pendulum) may have befitted the egocentric humanism of much of the Renaissance, but it missed the Hebrew-Christian perspective.

In his *Christmas Oratorio,* in many of his Cantatas, in the *B Minor Mass,* and in arias of *The Passion According to Saint Matthew* and *The Passion According to Saint John,* Bach also displayed what he sublimely summarized in his *Magnificat in D.* "Faith is the earnest of things hoped for."

No one can hear the *Sicut erat in principio* and believe that the Hellenized sage known as Ecclesiastes had the last word with his notorious exclamation, "All is vanity." The musical exegesis of the Leipzig master remains to this day the supreme exposition of a certitude that in Abraham and his universal progeny "all families of the earth shall seek and find their mutual welfare" (Gen 12:3).[4]

---

[4] According to Robert L. Marshall, Bach saw that the *Fecit potentiam* did not belong to the lines following but stands as "the home key at the midpoint of the whole composition. It begins in the subdominant and ends a fifth higher on the tonic . . . [The *Gloria Patri*] reintroduces the dominant . . . as the penultimate tonal moment of the work." But "the inevitable and definitive resolution of this harmony" is brought out by the *Sicut erat in principio (The Music of J. S. Bach,* Schirmer Books [New York: Macmillan, 1989], p. 169).

Contemplative Virgin

Available Recordings of the Magnificat

I. MIDDLE AGES

Gregorian Vespers
Johannes de Quatris (ca. 1350–1400)	Paris
Gilles Binchois (1400–1460)	Dijon
Guillaume Dufay (1400–1474)	Cambrai, Rome
Mikolaj de Radom (ca. 1450)	Cracow
Jacob Obrecht (1453–1505)	Utrecht, Cambrai, Antwerp
Pierre de La Rue (1460–1518)	Jena

II. SIXTEENTH CENTURY

Ludwig Senfl (ca. 1486–1543)	Wien, Innsbruck
Johannes Galliculus (ca. 1490–1550)	Leipzig
Cristobal de Morales (ca. 1500–1553)	Avila, Rome, Toledo
Thomas Tallis (1505–1585)	London
Thomas Appleby (ca. 1536)	Lincoln, Oxford
Andrea Gabrieli (1520–1586)	Venice
Giovanni da Pierluigi [Palestrina] (1525–1594)	Rome
Orlando de Lassus (1532–1594)	Rome, München
William Byrd (1543–1594)	London
Tomàs Luis de Victoria (1548–1611)	Rome
Luca Marenzio (1553–1599)	Rome

III. SEVENTEENTH CENTURY

Claudio Monteverdi (1567–1643)	Mantua
Heinrich Schütz (1585–1672)	Venice, Dresden
Zacharià̀s Zarevutis (ca. 1635–1665)	Bardejov
Jacek Rosycki (ca. 1697)	Warsaw, Dresden
Henry du Mont (1610–1684)	Paris
Marc-Antoine Charpentier (1634–1704)	Paris, Versailles
Dietrich Buxtehude (1637–1707)	Lübeck
Johann Pachelbel (1653–1706)	Nüremberg, Wien, Erfurt

IV. EIGHTEENTH CENTURY

Antonio Vivaldi (1678–1741)	Venice
Jan Dismas Zelenka (1679–1745)	Prague, Dresden
Georg Philipp Telemann (1681–1767)	Hamburg
Francisco António de Almeida (d. 1755)	Lisbon
Francesco Durante (1684–1755)	Naples
Johann Sebastian Bach (1685–1750)	Leipzig
Giovanni-Battista Sammartini (1701–1775)	Milan
Giovanni-Battista Pergolesi (1710–1736)	Naples
Baldassare Galuppi (1705–1785)	Venice
Carl Philipp Emanuel Bach (1714–1788)	Potsdam, Hamburg
Henri Hardouin (1727–1808)	Rheims
Wolfgang Amadeus Mozart (1756–1791)	Salzburg

V. NINETEENTH CENTURY

Franz Schubert (1797–1828)	Vienna
Franz Liszt (1811–1886)	Weimar, Rome

VI. TWENTIETH CENTURY

Ralph Vaughan Williams (1872–1958)	Cambridge
Michael Tippett (b. 1905)	Cambridge

Halsey Stevens (b. 1908)	Oberlin
Alan Hovhaness (b. 1911)	New York
Robert Caamaño (b. 1923)	Buenos Aires
Krzysztov Penderecki (b. 1933)	Cracow, New Haven
Paul Chihara (b. 1938)	New York, Los Angeles

Selected Bibliography on
the Magnificat in Music

Borren, C. van den, ed., *Polyphonia Sacra: A Continental Miscellany of the Fifteenth Century* (Burnham, Bucks., 1952).

Goldsmith, E. W., ed., *Fourteen Ancient Fauxbourdons Set to the Song of the Blessed Virgin Mary* (London, 1912).

Illing, C. H., *Zur Technik der Magnificat-Kompositionen des 16. Jahrhunderts* (Wolfenbüttel & Berlin, 1936).

Lerner, E. R., "The Polyphonic Magnificat in 15th-Century Italy," *The Musical Quarterly*, vol. L (1964), pp. 44–58.

Meinholz, J. *Untersuchungen zur Magnificat-Komposition des 15. Jahrhunderts* (Diss., Cologne, 1956).

Reese, G., "The Polyphonic Magnificat of the Renaissance as a Design in Tonal Centers," *Journal of the American Musicological Society*, XIII (1960), pp. 68–78.

Santucci, P., *La Madonna della Musica*, Vol. I (Bologna, 1983), pp. 410–418.

Schweitzer, A., *J. S. Bach*, tr. E. Newman (London, 1949), Vol. II, pp. 166–171.

Steiner, R., Kirsch, W., Bullivant, R., "Magnificat," *The New Grove's Dictionary of Music and Musicians* (London, 1980), Vol. XI, pp. 495–500.

Weinandt, E. A., "Magnificat," *Choral Music of the Church* (New York, 1965), pp. 121–135.

N.B. A musical analysis of J. S. Bach's *Grand Magnificat in D* may be found in Philipp Spitta, *Johann Sebastian Bach*, tr. by C. Bell and J. A. Fuller-Maitland (New York, 1951), II, pp. 374–383.

Index of Names

OTHER BOOKS BY SAMUEL TERRIEN

The Psalms and their Meaning for Today
Job: Poet of Existence
Lands of the Bible
Job: Commentaire
The Power to Bring Forth
The Shorter New Testament
The Elusive Presence: Toward a New Biblical Theology
Till the Heart Sings: A Biblical Theology of Manhood and
      Womanhood
The Image of Job from the Catacombs to Chagall:
      Artists as Biblical Interpreters, 1995–1996.
Les Psaumes: Commentaire littéraire et théologique (3 vols.), 1995–
      1996.